THE IMPOSSIBLE POSSIBILITY

KALOS

The word *kalos* (καλός) means beautiful. It is the call of the good; that which arouses interest, desire: "I am here." Beauty brings the appetite to rest at the same time as it wakens the mind from its daily slumber, calling us to look afresh at that which is before our very eyes. It makes virgins of us all, and of everything—there, before us, lies something that we never noticed before. Beauty consists in *integritas sive perfectio* (integrity and perfection) and *claritas* (brightness/clarity). It is the reason why we rise and why we sleep—that great night of dependence, one that reveals the borrowed existence of all things, if, that is, there is to be a thing at all, or if there is to be a person at all. Here lies the ground of all science, of philosophy, and of all theology, indeed, of our each and every day.

This series will seek to provide intelligent-yet-accessible volumes that have the innocence of beauty and of true adventure, and in so doing remind us all again of that which we took for granted, most of all thought itself.

SERIES EDITORS:
Conor Cunningham, Eric Austin Lee, and Christopher Ben Simpson

The Impossible Possibility

CHRIST AND THE PROBLEMS OF
FORGIVENESS

. . .

Caitlin Smith Gilson

With original art and contributions by
Carol Scott

CASCADE *Books* · Eugene, Oregon

THE IMPOSSIBLE POSSIBILITY
Christ and the Problems of Forgiveness

Kalos series

Copyright © 2024 Caitlin Smith Gilson. Artwork copyright © 2024 Carol Scott. All rights reserved. Except for brief quotations in critical publications or reviews, no part of this book may be reproduced in any manner without prior written permission from the publisher. Write: Permissions, Wipf and Stock Publishers, 199 W. 8th Ave., Suite 3, Eugene, OR 97401.

Cascade Books
An Imprint of Wipf and Stock Publishers
199 W. 8th Ave., Suite 3
Eugene, OR 97401

www.wipfandstock.com

PAPERBACK ISBN: 979-8-3852-2759-4
HARDCOVER ISBN: 979-8-3852-2760-0
EBOOK ISBN: 979-8-3852-2761-7

Cataloguing-in-Publication data:

Names: Smith Gilson, Caitlin [author]. | Scott, Carol [artist].

Title: The impossible possibility : Christ and the problems of forgiveness / Caitlin Smith Gilson ; with original artwork by Carol Scott.

Description: Eugene, OR: Cascade Books, 2024 | Series: Kalos | Includes bibliographical references and index.

Identifiers: ISBN 979-8-3852-2759-4 (paperback) | ISBN 979-8-3852-2760-0 (hardcover) | ISBN 979-8-3852-2761-7 (ebook)

Subjects: LCSH: Forgiveness. | Forgiveness—Biblical teaching. | Guilt. | Hope—Religious aspects—Christianity. | Theology, Practical. | Christian poetry, American. | Artwork.

Classification: BT790 S658 2024 (print) | BT790 (ebook)

Cover art, *Dome*, by Carol Scott. All poetry comes from Carol Scott and Caitlin Smith Gilson, *Heaven Sent: The Passion of the Last Words*. Kalos. Eugene, OR: Cascade, forthcoming 2025.

Thank you to Kyle Lundberg for his phenomenal cover design.

For Fred and our dearest children.

Long ago I was young
I did not know it then
But it was for you
To be this dying comet of love
Finishing my soul in you

I was created for you
Before you were born
Made by love for you
Created by you
This is how time works

What ends always begins again
The hours we have now
Have always been the only play
The only stage
The only way home

These hours together are my dying
These hours my conceiving
The curve of your cheek
Every nectar scented kiss
Your unmistakable face
I would know you in blindness
In the night of my mind
In you I have lived
Loved even more

I was born that day
Your touch encased me
Enclosed me in your littleness
You have been a rose
The bud of a rose
The remaining scent after the waterfall

And still you encase me now
That half of me halved again
That day

This my child, my little one
Is how time works
We are measured in giving
Time with you is my only dying
Loving you has been the only form of love
That is too good
To land anywhere on earth

Because of you
Even in the grave
I will float into sky and to river
Live my cherished one by water
So that I may come to you always —My Child, My Little One
for U.M.

Off the Rails, **by Carol Scott**

Table of Contents

Foreword, by Michael Carlin xi
    Passion. Art by Carol Scott xvi
Acknowledgments xvii
    Tongues of Fire. Art by Carol Scott xviii
Note on Art xix
    See No Evil. Art by Carol Scott xxi

Let This Cup Pass: Introductory Remarks on Forgiveness 1
    Sharing a Toast. Art by Carol Scott 1
    "The Mind of the Beloved." Poem by Caitlin Smith Gilson 2
    "Forgive Me." Poem by Carol Scott & Caitlin Smith Gilson 11
    Warhol Madonnas. Art by Carol Scott 12
    "The Legacy of Your Rosary." Poem by Caitlin Smith Gilson 13
1. Forgiveness: Four Difficulties Read through Euripides' *Medea* 15
    Let Them Eat Cake. Art by Carol Scott 15
    "All Your Light on Me." Poem by Carol Scott & Caitlin Smith Gilson 16
2. The Unknowing Heart of Forgiveness: The Problem of Hell 40
    Luminous Mysteries. Art by Carol Scott 40
    "Today I Was Late." Poem by Caitlin Smith Gilson 41
3. Three Mistaken Views on the Impossibility of Forgiveness 53
    The Muses. Art by Carol Scott 53
    "The Metaphysics of Love." Poem by Caitlin Smith Gilson 54
4. The Power of Christ's Forgiveness 60
    Crystal Fire. Art by Carol Scott 60
    "The Axe and Tear." Poem by Caitlin Smith Gilson 61

TABLE OF CONTENTS

5. Christ's Saving Love in His Seven Last Words 69
      The Dying God. Art by Carol Scott 69
      "My Secret." Poem by Caitlin Smith Gilson 70
      Goodbye Rain. Art by Carol Scott 77
      "Every Day Since You Were Born." Poem by Caitlin Smith Gilson 78

Bibliography 79
Index 85

Foreword

by Michael Carlin

"For if you forgive men their trespasses, your heavenly Father also will forgive you; but if you do not forgive men their trespasses, neither will your Father forgive your trespasses" (Matt 6:14–15). Christ does not so much make a case for the obligation to forgive as warn us of the inevitable consequences if we do not. The stakes could not be higher, and eternal life is warrant enough for any author to focus her gaze on this matter. But a philosopher? It is agonizingly clear that we cannot reason our way to forgiveness any more than a physicist can hope to hit fastballs thrown at him after plotting their precise trajectories. Philosophy may console, but it cannot convince a parent to forgive the man who victimized his child. Caitlin Smith Gilson is a distinctive voice within philosophy and begins her treatment of forgiveness with precisely this challenge to our pious (and necessary!) acceptance of our obligation to forgive. For anyone who has been deeply hurt by someone, Christ's injunction to forgive is both absurd and even sadistic, heaping as it does a further obligation on one who is already wounded, an obligation that carries the weight of sin for one who would neglect it.

Smith Gilson does not run from the pain endured by anyone who must forgive, nor does she wave away the pain with facile writerly paradox. Instead, she offers her reader a *paideia* in the demands and rights of the Christian who takes seriously his obligation to forgive. It is a true *paideia*— a formation in citizenship—that ignores none of the obligations taken on by those who would become citizens in the Heavenly Kingdom of the Pardoned. Although the Christian earnestly looks to eternity, the obligation to seek justice here and now is a preliminary requirement to even imagine forgiveness as genuine. It is stipulated: forgiveness in this world can never fully recover what sin has damaged or taken away. We can never be the same, but

FOREWORD

we can be made new as forgiveness conforms our hearts to God. Here then is the arena in which we are to confront forgiveness, the heart. Smith Gilson takes us through the permutations of the heart facing forgiveness, exploring some of the most critical challenges to Christian forgiveness along the way. Smith Gilson takes the criticisms on their own terms—this is no history of ideas that drains the venom from Nietzsche's frontal attack by endless contextualization. The wounded heart is not healed by such evasions.

Over the first three chapters, we confront the challenges set out by the most eloquent critics of forgiveness. In the first chapter we turn over the claims of Euripides' Medea for vengeance as a duty owed to justice. Four substantial claims are examined and, Smith Gilson states them in the most compelling terms. At one point, Smith Gilson clarifies Medea's motives: "... what drives her is objective justice, not mere personal offense. The question of atonement is far more serious than one of competing emotional stances" (25). Grounding Medea's struggle in the historical sublimation of vengeance as sacrifice, Smith Gilson sheds a startling light on Medea's homicidal rage: "Revenge though is not solely retaliatory. It also seeks to reform/teach the offender justice through a sheer experience of *how* the original offense was unjust. Vengeance is the punishment designed to express how much human beings abhor violence!" (25). Only by accompanying this wounded and vengeful victim can we appreciate the full weight of the claims against Christian forgiveness and therefore how distinctive and alien the call to forgive is to normal human sensibilities. In experiencing the full measure of her abandonment, Medea helps us see that there is no "worthy" object of forgiveness just as there is no "worthy" subject of forgiveness. Victims must take this by nature unjust obligation upon themselves or risk the promised superabundance of Christ's love. None of this makes sense as mere civic virtue or bland human decency.

In chapter 2, Smith Gilson takes us swiftly to the impossible model for all acts of forgiveness, the remission of sin effected in Christ's saving work. From a propaedeutic viewpoint this is not a useful example, for, to imitate Christ, we would have to reach back into the past and change "locked history" to cancel transgressions and make them count no longer as sins. Christ signals His realization of this impossible act with a similarly impossible gesture: in the moment of His greatest agony, Christ prays from the cross for the forgiveness of His tormentors: "Father forgive them for they know not what they do." The impossibility of this exemplary act was assailed by Nietzsche as an absurdity. If Jesus seeks His tormentors' pardon on grounds of their ignorance, is this not also the case for all sinners? In the Socratic tradition all evil-doers are in some measure ignorant of the true nature of reality. Further, if God, the ultimate guarantor of justice, forgives based on ignorance, who really maintains full agency in any act if we cannot even recognize the choice for evil as a culpable act? To Nietzsche, such a vision represents an impossibly high standard for guilt—we must know why we acted against our own self-interest after recognizing that we have done so. If civilized society accepts this standard for forgiveness between people then all individuals are drained of their vital principle and there is no opportunity for the great to exercise magnanimity and seek greatness in this life. One imagines Nietzsche himself nodding along to Smith Gilson's recapitulation of his case against Christian slave morality. Without giving the whole case away, the contingency Nietzsche sees in a Christian ethic of forgiveness is misunderstood when the full scope of Christ's saving work (realized in his humanity) is understood.

What of those who approach the obligation to forgive with good will and undertake it with their best abilities? In her third chapter, Smith Gilson examines three distinct pathologies in which forgiveness is approached as a function of our natural capacities. This is not a facile critique of moral Pelagianism, but rather a careful understanding of the ways the heart undertakes its proper work. The human heart was made, indeed was optimized, to forgive in precise measure that it was made to submit itself to the will of God, uniting its own efforts at forgiveness to God's saving will. The only real forgiveness is validated in the measure that we experience it as unachievable. Forgiveness that feels achievable is merely therapy.

In her final two chapters, Smith Gilson makes her turn to explore the work of Christ as Forgiver and its effect on the human heart. Christ's universal sacrifice breathes His Spirit through humanity, implicating us all in His love for each one. She examines one last failure of human forgiveness in the figure of Caligula from Albert Camus. In a last failed thrust, Caligula disposes of the classical inheritance of forgiveness as a function of magnanimity. Better the impossible than that. Only now can we accept our full dependence on Christ as enabling us to forgive. Smith Gilson fixes upon the seven last words of Christ from the cross as the definitive catechism on human forgiveness, since it is the moment when He realizes fully His self-emptying, by which we are filled with His love:

> Christ's entire self-emptying is the key to forgiving our sins. His totalizing sacrifice allows our most confused desires for forgiveness

> to be clarified and seen. Christ enters the depths of the impossible and the failed, and He subsumes that ignorance, impossibility, and failure within human language in its pure form spoken by God as Word. (71)

In human terms, forgiveness seems a bad-faith bargain, for it is all contingent, it all just "depends." We accept an obligation we are powerless to see through to its conclusion, but it is a bargain we make with a man crucified and expiring before our eyes. Smith Gilson reveals that this is the only kind of bargain we can make, and our only partner in the bargain is a dying man.

This contingency is mirrored in Smith Gilson's use of art and poetry in this meditation. Each reader must strike his own bargain with the poems and images on offer here. Art and poetry make their own non-negotiable demands upon the reader. Readers surrender their needs for precise significance and in return find experiences that deepen the text.

Passion, by Carol Scott

Acknowledgments

Many thanks to the marvelous editorial team at Wipf & Stock. Most particularly, Michael Thomson, Matthew Wimer, Zechariah Mickel, the remarkable Heather Carraher, and most especially Robin Parry, our brilliant and generous editor. Robin—your guidance and wisdom over the last few years have helped bring out the best in my work. I am blessed.

To my dear friend and writing partner Carol for all your genius, magnificent artistry in this book, and joyful faith. And to Susie Bear our dear friend in art.

Thank you Connie and Christian for your friendship and support for the arts!

To Fr. Labastida, Mike, Susan, Irina, Ashlinn, Bobby, Grace, Danny, Grace Gallaher, Aunt Nancy, Maria, Joseph Terry, Nicole, Todd, Erika, Philippe, Mark, Victoria, Elizabeth, Pam, and Cindy for all your love and support.

Michael—thank you for your friendship and for writing the foreword to this book in your inimitable style. It has been a true joy sharing the faith and teaching with you.

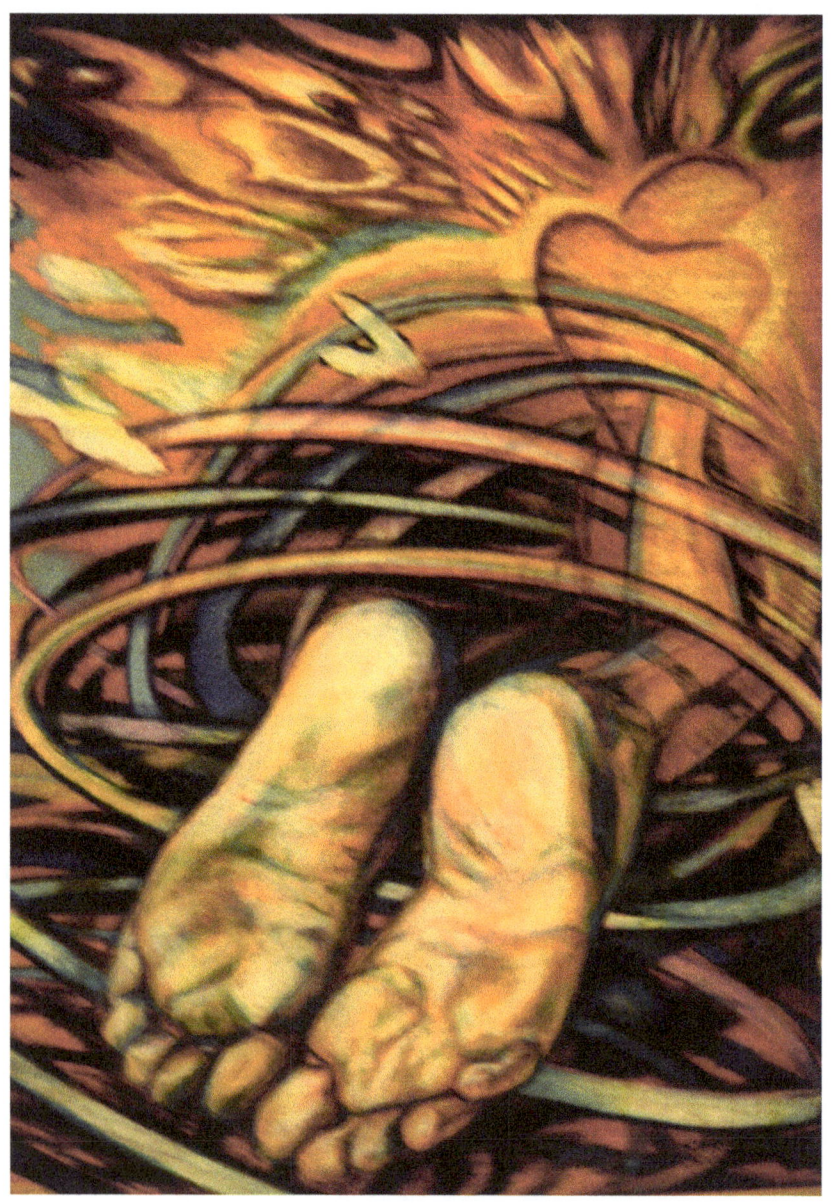

Tongues of Fire, by Carol Scott

Note on Art

All art in this volume is conceived and created by Gallery 600 Julia artist, Carol Scott. Carol is professor emeritus of art at the University of Holy Cross, New Orleans. She has had numerous one-person shows, has over six hundred artworks created, has exhibited in galleries and museums, has won awards, and is collected and commissioned nationally and internationally. She has been honored with a one-person show in New York City and a retrospective in New Orleans at THE BUILDING Arts Venue & Gallery, https://www.building1427.com/. The City of New Orleans selected her work for their permanent collection, and she has served as the vice president of the Women's Caucus for Art.

Carol co-authored two books of poetry and art with Caitlin Smith Gilson, *Rhapsody and Redolence: The Crystal Decade* (Cascade, 2024) and *Luminous Darkness: The Passion of the Last Words* (Cascade, 2025). Carol's work has also been selected for the prestigious Chianciano Biennale in Tuscany for leading international and contemporary artists.

To see her work visit the Gallery District in New Orleans (https://gallery600julia.com/carol-scott/) and her website: www.carolscottart.com.

> When I saw Carol Scott's paintings, my first impression was their wondrous intensity—bursting with joy! The colors are shockingly bold, and the things in the painting feel like they are in motion. For me, her art expresses both movement and stillness, almost shouting with gladness. Because of its subject matter—I am thinking here specifically of "Luminous Mysteries," but all her works have this element—her art shimmers with profundity, as Scott seems to have penetrated into the deepest energy and passion that pours forth from Christ's cross. I can't think of other artists whose works pulsate with the joy and energy of being, and with the "pouring

Note on Art

forth" or shouting with joy of sheer grace, that I find in Scott's best paintings, of which there are many.

—Matthew Levering, James N. Jr. and Mary D. Perry Chair of Theology, University of Saint Mary of the Lake, IL; editor, *Word on Fire: The New Ressourcement Journal*

See No Evil, by Carol Scott

Let This Cup Pass

Introductory Remarks on Forgiveness

Sharing a Toast, by Carol Scott

Your conscience, footfall in snow
Compressed crystal white under shadowless moonlight
I need your peerless curved singular feature pressed into form
Tread across my land infinite mind living inside this marooned need
Forgive me
Forgive this body and this mind
Forgive these thoughts, these things
Falling open exposed without cover your foolish lover
All matter and form crushed circulating the tear of instant ice
I will know all earths touched by you, I will bow at your shadows in play
If only you were endless day
My soul
My soul
If only the grace of your need
You dip into my snow, carving transferring shape
Your waveless light tapers the passageway of spliced lines, this trading of minds
Forgive me
All fire and love
All matter and form crushed circulating the tear of instant ice

—"The Mind of the Beloved," by Caitlin Smith Gilson

The Impossible Possibility of Forgiveness

> The Lord is not slack concerning his promise, as some count slackness, but is longsuffering toward us, not willing that any should perish but that all should come to repentance.
> —2 Peter 3:9

IF YOU GIVE THE question *"what is forgiveness?"* any real attention, then it is intolerable. Let us not dance around the issue or return to the depository of thoughtlessness by reducing Christ to a fantasy figure who makes all things as they were. The truth of the matter is that the acts most in need of forgiveness are the very ones unable to be recovered. This reality remains unchanged; faith is not a parlor trick. Christ descended into hell because terrible evils in need of forgiveness are deeper than death. He rose with gaping wounds because we are dealing with an unimaginable rescue mission. If we shortcut the wild impossible possibility of forgiveness, we vacate the audacity of Christian faith and the very groundwork for real belief.

Forgiveness may well be getting away with murder, the undoing of what is final and cannot be undone. Take away the abstract hypotheticals, return yourself to the concrete situation of the dead child mutilated on the ground. Now it is your child, a bloodied caricature of former life, mangled and collapsed. Bear for a moment the impossible weight of what this means. You, shipwrecked in grief—a living death—are given yet another cruelty added to the absurdity, heaped atop the loss. You are tasked with forgiving the one who wielded the hammer. Do not stray from reality. Your child's head caved in with the same force of a smashed melon, all that promise already decomposing.

But your task to forgive is *not* the impossible possibility of forgiveness. In your sleep and your waking, call to mind the vision of your dead child. Those unblinking eyes, which had not seen enough or experienced the world, are staring back from the void. His defeated body, all blood, water, and substance, sinking into the concrete. In that entanglement of sight and night, you realize you do not have the right even to forgive.

Never forget that it is not *your* life snatched away. You are not yet inside a closed casket below the earth, you still live and breathe. What does this mean but that another power has been taken from you. You do not have the right to forgive the taking of this life. It is not your life, it was your child's, his future, and his to forgive. But your child, the one who has such rights, is mute, deep in death, a broken defeated body with no voice to offer or refuse forgiveness. This means what it has always meant: forgiveness is impossible. Impossible in more than one respect. The killer may not ask for forgiveness and what is to be done then? There is the death of the body but also the deadlier death of the soul. Without repentance, this most final death is already occurring in the killer. Even if he seeks forgiveness, the impossibility of its completion is lodged squarely at the center of his repentance. The one who *could* forgive him is dead—he took two lives that day, the child's and his own. His own life—body and soul—is in protracted dying.

For forgiveness to be truly good and just, it necessitates a sacred capacity well beyond what is understandable in the here and now. *Forgive us our trespasses, forgive us our debts*: we mouth these words and rarely acknowledge their very high price. The guttural cries of grief and guilt may circle the truth, but only by way of exile. All salvation is the holding together of opposing poles that must come together, but we have no power to unite them. A mortal woman gave life to God, Christ is fully God and fully man, and death is the inconceivable way to life. These polar realities come together only *through* forgiveness as their electrifying core. How can we believe it all to be possible? But we must believe. It is necessary for our eternal life and happiness. It is all or nothing.

Forgiveness is both *impossible* and *necessary*. Terrible unobtainable demands are placed on each of us to accomplish this task, which from the outset, make no mistake, is an impossible one. What we sense in our trespasses is the essential need to forgive. For without its redemptive recovery, a soul is lost. In fact, all souls are lost without forgiveness. Neither man nor God can love perfectly and completely if one of us perishes entirely. Forgiveness alone saves the lost, and it is simultaneously beyond our grasp. This unreachability never retreats into abstraction. It is an infuriating nonstarter that demands more of the innocent than the guilty, more of the one in the wreckage of ruptured love than the one who commits evil. For the time being, we may content ourselves that forgiveness is defined as a change in attitude, but that does not satisfy. We may do good or evil with positive spirits, but good and evil are *still* accomplished. To forgive is no mere change in attitude, even if that change toward peace gives blessed relief.

How and when is forgiveness possible or preferable and when is it just and good? There are hurdles to climb, and miles to go before we sleep, and questions with elusive answers. We face the risk that more insurmountable issues will arise, and many will go unresolved. The question of forgiveness is far more grave than any of us would like to admit; for we are all sinners and each of us ill-equipped to offer what we so lack and need. Again, how can we give to others what we dearly need ourselves? And we need it to survive . . . .

Only one person has risen from the dead to forgive our sins, and to recover in a new form that which is lost. Without Christ, we are powerless to undo and retrieve what has been destroyed. It is irrevocable. If this is the case, what then does human forgiveness do in our present life? Why are we tasked with its weighted and impossible features if it appears we only have the power to change our state of mind and not the state itself? Anything can change our state of mind—denial, drugs, social views. But we seek a real and redemptive *recovery*, which is the meaning and heart of forgiveness.

Christianity has always been a scrambling to meet God face to face *while* knowing we haven't the power to achieve this most precious love and vision. And yet, impossibly so, we have *already* received that love and forgiveness. We navigate these two poles as we live, and neither cancels the other. To strain and fail to accomplish forgiveness, and to be forgiven: this is the anguish and beauty of Christianity. We must absorb this teaching and its mystery into our bodies and souls.

> If your brother or sister sins against you, rebuke them; and if they repent, forgive them. Even if they sin against you seven times in a day and seven times come back to you saying "I repent," you must forgive them.
> —Luke 17:3–4

Preliminary Ideas of Forgiveness: Separating the Wheat from the Chaff

> Christ emphasizes so insistently the need to forgive others that when Peter asked Him how many times he should forgive his neighbor He answered with the symbolic number of "seventy times seven" (Mt. 18:22), meaning that he must be able to forgive everyone every time. It is obvious that such a generous requirement of forgiveness does not cancel out the objective requirements of justice. Properly understood, justice constitutes, so to speak, the goal of forgiveness. In no passage of the Gospel message does forgiveness, or mercy as its source, mean indulgence towards evil, towards scandals, towards injury or insult. In any case, reparation for evil and scandal, compensation for injury, and satisfaction for insult are conditions for forgiveness.
> —Pope John Paul II, *Dives in Misericordia*

In the Gospels, it is abundantly clear Christ commands us to forgive. We cannot withhold forgiveness from the one who snatches our happiness, destroys our peace, or even extinguishes the unrepeatable life that grew inside our bellies and who was the sunrise every day. We must relinquish the one power we have left—*the refusal to forgive*. When we decline to forgive, we play a hand in directing the killer toward the abyss and to its dissevering of life and hope.

From justice *alone* doesn't the killer deserve my rejection and its punitive consequences? Doesn't his terrible crime—in which my child will never dance or play or marry—demand my refusal to forgive? My spurning of any atonement may issue in the killer receiving a proper reflection of his evil—the terminal end of his own possibilities. But this is not Christ's injunction. His incarnation is the heartbreaking unity of justice *and mercy*. Our Lord is the only human born to die for it takes a sacrifice deeper than death to recover what by the natural order would be forever lost. Forgiveness reminds us that Christ comes to save all of us. We are each unworthy, each human being is a broken creature once made perfectly by God's love.

The poles of tension that characterize the dynamite heart of Christianity ensure that our thinking remains thoughtful, intensively reflective, and nuanced. Genuine forgiveness is always anchored in Christ as just and merciful. There is no justice devoid of mercy nor are there merciful acts that are unjust. True justice is merciful and true mercy is just. This means that the obligation of justice and mercy must be fulfilled for the act of forgiveness to be genuine. It would be a violation of justice not to fight against terrorists or the Nazis. This is a misconstrued view of Christian forgiveness tethered to a hyperbolic understanding of mercy. *Turn the other cheek* is not indifference, passivity, or inaction. Our duty to forgive should never be confused with condoning evil. Nor should the demands of justice be tempted to ignore the call to mercy. Each of us understands the event that appears "unforgivable," from murders, to genocide, to pedophile priests. But to go down that road of the *unforgivable* means that mercy is congealed and hardened. Soon, far more quickly than we ever imagine, mercy is nowhere to be found, and mercy is essential to this life and the next. Christian forgiveness is neither extreme, for it neither reflects the wisdom of Christ nor the rescue mission of salvation through which grace and our free will *must* work in unison. This cooperation shows that forgiveness begins in mercy—we do not know fully what we have do—and through that mercy Christ's grace is effective. Forgiveness *always* requires our free will, as the gift of salvation can be accepted or refused. Any situation where free will is involved so too is justice:

> For if you forgive men their trespasses, your heavenly Father also will forgive you; but if you do not forgive men their trespasses, neither will your Father forgive your trespasses.
> —Matthew 6:14–15

Forgiveness Is Not Opposed to Anger

Forgiveness is not opposed to anger nor is it primarily about feelings. Again, the actions most in need of forgiveness are those impossible to forgive. Christ's death and descent into the spiritual annihilation of hell were necessary to accomplish genuine transformative forgiveness. Though anger itself is not a sin, sometimes it may be a propaedutic to or a detractor from forgiveness. But forgiveness itself is emphatically something *more* and other. No emotion can achieve forgiveness; even if anger profoundly reveals to us how much is amiss and awry, it can never resolve and recover what is lost. It too is powerless.

> Be angry but do not sin; do not let the sun go down on your anger.
> —Ephesians 4:26

We see the paradox of anger in relation to forgiveness. There is justifiable anger, as Christ overturns the tables in the temple. Anger often inflames the desire for objective justice, for the essential atonement needed for forgiveness to materialize. But anger, while justifiable, rarely can be acted upon without descending into a sinful and retributive response. We are to *be* angered when that is the right response. St. Thomas Aquinas calls such anger praiseworthy. But we are also to let it pass as the sun goes down. Understood properly, anger points to the supernatural need for Christ. It may illuminate the moral problem, but it cannot rectify it, it has no ability to issue the genuine recovery of what is lost. Anger gets us to the limits of our own human, societal, and earthly powers to effect change. Our outrage unveils our lack of self-sufficiency. But indignation can easily forget itself and vainly attempt to rectify what it cannot fix, becoming inordinate and unjust, unraveling family and social structures. Even in this, anger shows the truth: we have not the capacity to complete the task of forgiveness. We need Christ.

We desire a return to the beginning, to put all the pieces back on the chessboard, a restart and reboot of choices, situations, and relationships. But the die has been cast, and in the interplay of freedom and circumstances, ill feelings may not go away, and trust may not easily return. Indeed, we know it is right and just to love the sinner not the sin. Prudence, therefore, may designate a guardedness when revisiting those who have sinned repeatedly against us or we them. It would be unwise and immoral to treat the serial rapist as if he had never committed his crimes, that is a pseudo attempt to recover *what was*. Understanding the trespasser's predilections may help prevent other victims and curb sin and the fallout from sin. We do not retreat into abstractions. Forgiveness refuses such moves. The impossible possibility of forgiveness is at the heart of all Christian teaching. Christ risks it all to recover what is lost, and while we are not worthy to assist Him, He asks for us to do just that—to forgive *with* and *through* Him.

Forgiveness Is Not Returning to the Past

If the past is a foreign country and they do things differently there, then going home to how the relationship was in the past, before the rupture from sin, is never quite going home! We cannot retrieve this prior and happy state. In all sin we are reminded of the exile from the Garden. Every evil action is another departure from the Eden of *once was*. With Adam and Eve, we are now on a longer and more fraught way to heaven. Trust was given to us, and we broke it. To give it again by ignoring our offenses would be unjust and unmerciful on God's part. The same principle holds in human relationships fractured by sin. We have violated trust; it is only just we work to earn it. It is only merciful that we are granted a new compact in trust knowing full well we never quite recover *what was*. There are partial recoveries on earth, new avenues to grow and deepen, but full recovery is only possible in heaven and even then, it is also in a new way, and a new form.

Forgiveness Is Not an Emotional Perspective

Forgiveness, to be more than an improvement in emotional perspective, necessitates three parties: the trespasser, the trespassed against, and Christ. In His mercy, because Christ *is* God, when we are with Him, we may be forgiven. The audacity of the incarnation, passion, and resurrection is that Christ takes into Himself *all* things. He knows each of us more than ourselves, and we are transfigured through His love. But faith is always this balancing of polar realities. Christians on earth live within the impossibility of completing forgiveness and within its completion *through* the body of Christ. To be Christians we enact both realities and neither on earth cancels out the other.

Christ Requires More Than Preemptive Forgiveness

We can never settle for an easy preemptive forgiveness, which may have good intentions but may shortcut the obligations of justice and Christ's redemptive grace. As much as we would like to have a preemptive forgiveness, where either I forgive myself for my sin or I forgive the other for his sin independent of the act of contrition, these choices undermine the reality that none of us is self-sufficient. We need the other person in the relationship who has offended us or we him. Otherwise how is forgiveness anything other than a change in emotional disposition and with no reference to the other party? We require the other to enter a forgiveness that recovers what is lost and by Christ's grace offers even more. In preemptive forgiveness we are hitting at potentially noble actions, foreshadowing the power of forgiveness, but it cannot take the place of Christ. When we have an attitude to forgive or to seek forgiveness, we may be engaging in virtue training, such as tempering our anger, curbing our pride, and working on humility. But Christ never demands unconditional forgiveness. The condition is that the other has repented. You are right to reproach the trespasser, but *if* there is repentance you must forgive. That *if* is the condition and the relationship required to effect real forgiveness.

Having an attitude toward forgiveness—such as patience, understanding, charity, and love—renders you ready to offer the great gift that assists in raising us as brothers and sisters in heaven, and not strangers and enemies in hell. While this inclination can be virtuous it must also be prudent, never sinking into ignoring the sin. This is neither just nor merciful as it leaves open the door to repeated sinful acts. The *desire* to forgive should be unconditional. We must always want the best for others and forgiveness is the *only* gateway to heaven. But the demand for unconditional and preemptive forms of forgiveness are another matter altogether. If God enacted unconditional and preemptive forgiveness, indifferent to any acts of contrition, neither would it be just and merciful nor would there be any teachings on hell. But we know differently:

> The Son of man shall send forth his angels, and they shall gather out of his kingdom all things that offend, and them which do iniquity; and will cast them into the furnace of fire. There will be wailing and gnashing of teeth.
> —Matthew 13:41–42

We need forgiveness; many of us have fallen out of a state of grace and are unwilling to repent. If Christ demanded preemptive and unconditional forgiveness, all would be in a state of grace for in essence there would be nothing to forgive! This is plainly absurd and undercuts the great sacrifice Christ paid for us. Christ's death never violates our free will. The admission price of salvation is forgiveness, to forgive and to be forgiven. The great transformation of our hearts and minds in their glorified state requires this union of grace and free will enacted throughout our lives. Christ's gift to us on the cross is not a sleight of hand where all are saved once and subsequently all can do as they please. This is why our Lord's daily prayer reminds us: "forgive us our trespasses as we forgive those who trespass against us."

> Christianity, true, as always, to the complexity of the real, presents us with something knottier and more ambiguous—a God so full of mercy that He becomes man and dies by torture to avert that final ruin from His creatures, and who yet, where that heroic remedy fails, seems unwilling, or even unable, to arrest the ruin by an act of mere power. I said glibly a moment ago that I would pay "any price" to remove this doctrine. I lied. I could not pay one-thousandth part of the price that God has already paid to remove the fact. And here is the real problem: so much mercy, yet still there is Hell.
> —C. S. Lewis, *The Problem of Pain*

Forgiveness Recovers the Image of God in Our Hearts

We forgive and ask for forgiveness so that we may recover the image of God in our hearts and minds. Christ became human and died for us so that the image of grace and eternal life we exiled in original sin can be gifted to us again in a new form, in the God-Man, who takes on our sins. Christ loves the sinner while overcoming the death at root in all sin. The unveiled, renewed, and recovered image of God is to love through suffering, to love the sinner and to overcome the death at root in the sin. We must *seek* to forgive, in seeking we shall find that we are children of God in heaven:

> But I say to you, love your enemies, bless those who curse you, do good to those who hate you, and pray for those who spitefully use you and persecute you, that you may be sons of your Father in heaven; for he makes his sun rise on the evil and on the good, and sends rain on the just and on the unjust.
> —Matthew 5:44–45

Forgiveness is no mere change in attitude, it is the difference between life and death, between heaven and the second death of hell. The loss of forgiveness is the disintegration of the saving image of God. Without mercy and justice, we spiral to the root of sin, which is permanent death. We desire the good of every soul, even and especially those most lost and entrenched in evil. If we knew what hell truly is, we would never wish it on our own worst enemy. Hell, as we shall see, is not the death of the body but the death of the soul. We forgive and hope in God's forgiveness so that all may see us truly overcome in grace and the joy of eternal life. Forgive me so that I may love truly and be saved. Forgive me so that I may see you, Lord, as you are, as I am, as we are, and love all as you do.

Would you unpin my mortal dress in the shadow?
As if this sky we share is made of thousands of silver rings
And the edges of my undone dress flow into its cylinder canopy
Your Word wills the sacred rotation held past forgetting
And your touch the intrinsic wilderness retreating into my present tense
Would you take apart the things that hold me together?
I need you
I wade into the stream of your ether
And I need you over and under my unfastened body
Dropped down into concentric rings of this spiraling
All sighs and veils
From the golden crown down the bony spine
I am solid
Bending from waist to toe
Fitting the shape of you
The shade of your color
The muscle of your vibrations
Our currents flow
Electrified
Promise of rose buds bloom
Imagined utopia
I understand much and little
I understood what it is to die
To desire what is past sleeping
The innocence of the silent night
The gentle earth
I need you
And you forgive me

—"Forgive Me" by Carol Scott & Caitlin Smith Gilson

Warhol Madonnas, by Carol Scott

Crown of Roses, your design, a decade of you
Consuming fire of sight, entwined plight of the Holy night
No one can do what you have done
Garland infinity, legacy of life, Annunciation, Fruit the Mystery
Fruit of you, Your art of love, the birth of Our Savior, heaven above
She veiled in sky blue cloak, blessing us, Her perfected tear, diamond beads
    pressed from coal
Miraculous movement, say the Word, satisfy our soul, The waters of the
    Jordan
Flowing wine of Cana Fruit of the Mystery, Fruit of you, Your art of love
Transfigured bodies, Your innocence on my lips
I am not worthy say the Word, hell below, heaven above
This faith, into the muscle of your finger touch, I think of the heart of you
    weeping
At the foot of the cross, the anguish in the garden, haunting scent of wilting
    flower
Lying lifeless world, False gods, False power, the scourging at the pillar
Fruit of the Mystery, Fruit of you, Your art of love, blood red thorns
Contemptuous world, cross and death, hell below, no heaven above
O my Jesus, my Christ, this Child, forgive us, save us from the fire of hell
Lead all souls to heaven, especially those who are most in need
Reworked loss into glowing time, each bead a glimpse of the divine
Sparks of your seamless heart, all light inside dreamless globes . . .
Forever imperishable fire, angels engulfed in pearl, drowned in the blood of
    the Lamb
Crystalline white and pink, olive seed from the Garden of Gethsemane
Your perfect art, Your legacy of love
No one can do what you have done
Press the crucifix to my lips into the ghost of me, shining mystery of your
    incarnate rosary

—"The Legacy of Your Rosary" (excerpt) by Caitlin Smith Gilson

The Impossible Possibility

I accuse myself of having prayed but little or badly for the dead, of having thought of them only on certain days and along with the crowd, forgetting that they may need me every moment of the day, that they are more defenseless than children and that our thoughts should never abandon their painful cradle: forgetting that every single one of the dead needs every single one of us, and that a collective homage does not abate their suffering, which is still more individually felt than the suffering of the living. . . . I accuse myself of having practically forgotten the Dogma of Purgatory, of not having realized to what an extent it reveals the splendour of the divine justice, of not having realized that a too earthly soul, having caught a glimpse of heaven, itself experiences the admirable necessity of preparing itself the better therefore *by purifying itself*—that the dead are very great souls, which consider themselves not beautiful enough for the beauty of God, and which, like the Saints on Earth, but more than the Saints, are consumed with a sublime ferocity of desire to eradicate every imperfection in themselves and to burn the old Adam. . . . I accuse myself of having, in my own heart, allowed the dead to die.

—Jacques Debout, *My Sins of Omission*

1

Forgiveness

FOUR DIFFICULTIES READ THROUGH EURIPIDES' *MEDEA*

Let Them Eat Cake, by Carol Scott

The Impossible Possibility

I love the sunshine, it could be that my hair is made of some ancient form of its burnt out dust
And like the sun becoming gentler, lighter, softer in you, I am missing you
It is settling in, the ache
Even in the morning, when I do not wish to wake, I feel the life of the sun on me
The shining presence unmoved by time, the sun moves unspent bodies into unspoken grace
I feel haunted by the whole reality of you, you are eclipse itself hovering over my senses
Cover me, uncover me, I need your moving light and shadow
I miss the atmosphere of you, the way you caress the sunlight, how it pours off your skin
My long gold draping your back, this contrast is the all-loving slide of my lips taking you in
Squeezed citrus crisp fall, time of our past, time recalled, I am missing you
It is settling in, the ache, my soul stretches back to you, knotted up in you
Your kisses as sunshine, dreaming our bodies renewed in time, your skin, glowing in all seasons
My body brought into reason, the double ache of you eclipsing me, I will dream tonight
Your kiss as moonbeam, I will dream of the food of your soul
The food of your body dreaming of mine, I have felt sunset, the day one dies
When it is done, but you eclipse the sun, I will dream tonight, your kiss as moonbeam
I am coming home, I want to watch the sun move over you, all of you in one long unbroken day
You into me, beyond the sun, I wish the night remained the night, and you remained with me
My hair falling on your body, my life flowing into your body, everything I am
Floating into you, the double ache of you eclipsing me, once again shadows dancing in the dark
It was just a moment ago of exquisite joy manifested love
Gold turns to yellow roses with fragrant blooms, petals falling on and on
There are many bodies, but yours is the only one that holds your soul, my soul
I pray for the moments yet to come, I remember

—"All Your Light on Me," by Carol Scott & Caitlin Smith Gilson

> Therefore, if you are offering your gift at the altar and there remember that your brother or sister has something against you, leave your gift there in front of the altar. First go and be reconciled to them; then come and offer your gift.
> —Matthew 5:23–24

As CHRIST IS HUNG on the cross, His first saying is one of forgiveness. As Son, He asks with all children that our Father forgives us. *We do not know what we do.* This is one of the most enigmatic sayings in the Gospel and central to the drama of salvation. There is no salvation, no heaven, no resurrection, no eternal happiness without forgiveness. The Son of Man offers up His Spirit so that we may recover our true home, heaven. He descends into abandonment, suffering every human cruelty to the bitter end. Before Christ makes this ultimate sacrifice, He lays the possibility of our recovery on forgiveness. To glimpse how heaven visited earth, we must understand the nature of forgiveness, separating the wheat from the chaff. We must distinguish genuine lifesaving forgiveness from the many false alternatives. These problematic substitutes work against the genuine experiences of guilt, penance, peace, and surrender. A mismanaged view of forgiveness is a symptom of an emptied heaven, and even of hell on earth. We will diagnose and examine four difficult claims regarding forgiveness and penance. Let us see which help reveal our human nature, and which ones block the way. We hope to come closer to understanding the forgiveness Christ offers us as the way to salvation and happiness.

Before proceeding, let us take a quick look at a passage from Chekhov's short story *The Student*:

> The student thought again that if Vasilisa wept and her daughter was troubled, then obviously what he had just told them, something that had taken place nineteen centuries ago, had a relation to the present—to both women, and probably to this desolate village, to himself, to all people. If the old woman wept, it was not because he was able to tell it movingly, but because Peter was close to her, and she was interested with her whole being in what had happened to Peter's soul. And joy suddenly stirred in his soul, and he even stopped for a moment to catch his breath. The past, he thought, is connected with the present in an unbroken chain of events flowing one out of the other. And it seemed to him that he had just seen both ends of that chain: he touched one end, and the other moved.
> —Anton Chekhov, *The Student*

The past is always connected to the present, and to the future. A past event is not forgiven merely because it is the long-ago past. As we approach this chapter, let us acknowledge that our actions are deeply entwined in the lives of others. We interiorize and exteriorize the self and the beloved. This continual process throughout history reflects our universal community. We are all brothers and sisters and responsible for others. This reality gives profound credence to original sin as a wound spread through all generations. The past, with Chekhov, is never disconnected from us. Therefore, our desire for forgiveness and for salvation must extend to all.

Listed below are four alternatives when confronted with giving and receiving forgiveness. We will skirt the surface of this difficulty, then enter the depths, and play devil's advocate. Our goal is to reveal the rigorous forgiveness that Christ's offers on our behalf:

1. Why can't we resent and hold the grudge as recognition of injustice against us? Why is resentment bad? Why is forgiveness the unqualified good?
2. Why should I ask people to forgive me when I commit injustice?
3. If a person is guilty, what is the point of forgiving that other; that person's guilt needs to be settled through his/her own actions not mine. Is my forgiveness unjust? Am I prematurely extinguishing the just experience of guilt in the one who is guilty?
4. Shouldn't forgiveness be utterly gratuitous, but then what does it add to the situation, if utterly gratuitous? Perhaps, instead, forgiveness should be utilitarian.

Why Can't We Resent and Hold the Grudge?
(Or isn't the grudge a solid recognition of injustice against us? Why is resentment bad? Why is forgiveness the unqualified good?)

> All this, to me, is the "humanitarianism" of Christianity! Parasitism as the only practice of the church; with its anemic and "holy" ideals, sucking all the blood, all the love, all the hope out of life; . . . against health, beauty, well-being, intellect, kindness of soul—against life itself.
> —Friedrich Nietzsche, *The Antichrist*

What is the worth of adopting Christian values concerning forgiveness? Doesn't Christian morality expose us to more pain, deception, distrust, and with little gain? We have been taught to view the grudge as bad and forgiveness as the goal. On the other hand, resentment is a force strong enough to ensure we stick to so-called healthy boundaries. When we experience anger and resentment toward another person, it provides the essential space to process. Resentment allows us to avoid additional hurt and to reevaluate the relationship. When we take the "noble or high road," we are constantly attempting to experience what the other person is experiencing. We thwart the potentially positive aspects of the grudge conditioned to believe it is bad for our emotional health. Does the "high road" cause us to neglect the time needed to orient and know ourselves? Forgiveness requires us to put ourselves in the experience of others. But this may have a negative consequence. Are we failing to learn what actions we should and should not bear? Perhaps by *not* holding the grudge, we are promoting anemic ideals that will only fester in the long run. Does forgiveness suck all the healthy and honest instincts out of human experience? Does the grudge, in all its anger, allow us to develop some self-love rather than problematic self-pity?

In Euripides' *Medea*, the heart of the tragedy is the anger and rage of Medea, a jilted and betrayed wife. The very power of anger gives Medea the strength to calculate levels of revenge that will destroy everything in her wake, including her own children. She punishes cowardly Jason for his shamelessness. Medea learns from her unfaithful husband, Jason, that he is arranging to marry Glauce, princess of Corinth, daughter of King Creon. To avoid Medea's wrath and her powers as a sorceress, King Creon arranges to send Medea into exile. Jason's shameless rationale for this betrayal is the opportunity to elevate his standing. How can he pass up the opportunity to marry royalty? Medea is a barbarian, but Glauce is a princess. Only through Glauce can his family elevate their social standing. Jason blocks any passageway into redemption through a glut of promises: to keep her as a mistress, to figure a way to unite the families, to take care of her and the children, that he will not disown them. He experiences no guilt, asks for no forgiveness. In essence, what is the use or advantage for Medea of attempting to forgive him?

> Worst of the Worst! I can say only this, the greatest insult I can offer for your cowardice. You have come here, my bitterest enemy, here. There is no sign of boldness or of courage, to stand and face the family you have wronged. It's the worst of all human diseases: shamelessness.
> —Medea to Jason, *Medea*

The Impossible Possibility

Medea does not see how she will profit from ending her anger as Jason entreats her to do. This question of *profit* is the prime issue. In which respect does she profit from forgiving Jason, who does not feel shame and who is benefiting from his shameless actions? What choice or choices allow justice to take effect? How is it fair for Medea to bear the brunt of Jason's trickery dressed up as generosity?

> I'm not going to debate you anymore. If you want to accept the help my money can give you and the children in your exile, say so. I'm prepared to give without stint. I'll send tokens to my friends; they'll treat you well. You are a fool woman, if you're not willing to take it. You'll profit more if you end your anger.
> —Jason to Medea, *Medea*

Medea sees her vengeance supported by the gods. She is not only justifiable in anger, but justifiable in vengeance. This is the difficulty: the offender should know not abstractly but genuinely, in his spirit and marrow, the pain of being the author of injustice. Without this real felt knowledge, the offender cannot learn. We can view this avenging the wrong in two ways: (1) as justice that is instructive and necessary, or (2) an unjust revenge that further damages the delicate balances of human relationships. What then is the difference between the two, keeping in mind the education of the offender? It seems that justice requires:

a) a *proportionate* response to the offense;

b) the punishment given to the offender is properly measured out by proper figures in society, by God, so that it can instruct and elicit moral virtue;

c) the offender must genuinely understand the damage the sin/offense has caused to understand why it must be avoided.

Whereas unjust vengeance promotes:

a) a *disproportionate* response exceeding the parameters of the offense;

b) is handed out in a way that exceeds the authority of the person;

c) disproportionate suffering, which overwhelms any moral lesson; the unjust punishment cannot teach.

We now play devil's advocate. If someone callously murders an innocent person, why is execution of the offender unjust? Why do we consider castration for the repeat rapist unjust? Why do we think it justice to give the pedophile a twenty-year prison sentence when the child can never recover what is lost, no matter how many years? Forgiveness is also the issue. What does the victimizer's penance accomplish? Does the contrition undo the rape or the murder, does it recover what is lost? Our earthly justice carries more than a whiff of illegitimacy.

More still, these scenarios appear disproportionate. If the difference between a just and unjust action is rooted in a *proportionate* response to the offense, then is not the execution of the murderer a proportionate response? The jail sentence and pardon for child abuse seems terribly disproportionate, given what is taken away from the child. Again, does the redeemed offender make any difference to the situation? It cannot change what transpired, it cannot itself heal the victim. Even if a victimizer's contrition does help, contrition and justice should not be so conflated that the demands of justice are lessened, even circumvented. Isn't the victim the *most* knowledgeable as to when the demands of justice are met, when the punishment is proportionate to the offense? We see this terrible difficulty in Dostoevsky's magnum opus:

> I don't want the mother to embrace the oppressor who threw her son to the dogs! She dare not forgive him! Let her forgive him for herself, if she will, let her forgive the torturer for the immeasurable suffering of her mother's heart. But the sufferings of her tortured child she has no right to forgive; she dare not forgive the torturer, even if the child were to forgive him! And if that is so, if they dare not forgive, what becomes of harmony? Is there in the whole world a being who would have the right to forgive and could forgive? I don't want harmony. From love for humanity I don't want it. I would rather be left with the unavenged suffering. I would rather remain with my unavenged suffering and unsatisfied indignation, even if I were wrong. Besides, too high a price is asked for harmony; it's beyond our means to pay so much to enter on it. And so I hasten to give back my entrance ticket, and if I am an honest man I am bound to give it back as soon as possible. And that I am doing. It's not God that I don't accept, Alyosha, only I most respectfully return him the ticket.
> —Fyodor Dostoevsky, *The Brothers Karamazov*

If we avoid these difficulties, how can we envision heaven as anything other than the scrap heap for unresolved justice, love, and harmony? Earth and its passengers are on a journey. Heaven is supposed to be the welcome home that resolves all earthly failings, recovers what is lost. But this cannot be accomplished in an untrue, fantastical way. It is the mystery that fulfills every worthwhile yearning. We cannot neglect the dirty and difficult business of life. The proportionate justice that can elicit within the offender a remorseful recognition of his evil action is no easy feat. Especially for one steeped in lies and self-delusion. This *proportionate* response is full of risks. The cycle of justice is costly. We are so entrenched in original sin that we can never excise ourselves from it.

When we weigh these layered conflicts, Medea has a point. She has a valid reason for her desire for justice. She is right that it will take *much* for Jason to feel guilty for his actions. But Medea quickly transgresses into unjust vengeance. How does this happen? Her response to Jason's shamelessness is evil. She poisons Jason's father-in-law and new wife and murders her own children. These actions are in no way proportionate and just. Still, we take a closer look at this whole question. Why did Medea feel driven to such lengths in her quest for justice?

The genesis of anger in the tragedy foreshadows what is to come. Medea is filled with heavy-hearted anger. This is the type of anger that refuses at its core to accept the insults, the belittling, the diminishment Jason places upon her. Jason has wronged Medea, their children, and the bond they forged. He has abandoned his family, as if they had never played a consequential role in his life. Medea recognizes this and sees her anger as justifiable. She left her homeland Colchis. There she was considered a semi-divine royalty descended from the Sun God Helios. She left behind that prestige to marry Jason. Medea is exiled from Colchis having helped Jason obtain the Golden Fleece, preventing him from dying. She betrayed and killed her own family and people to protect Jason's life. Medea gave him children, which she rightly considers a fundamental gift, and the mark of their indelible bond.

Jason's responses only inflame Medea's justifiable anger. He claims:

A. *Medea is irrational*: he argues that Medea's whole exile and situation could have been avoided if she was not so unreasonable;

B. *he is generous*: that the marriage to Glauce (while still married to Medea) raises their children's social standing, placing them in the orbit of royalty;

C. *he has no obligation toward Medea*: Jason tells Medea that all the sacrifices she made for him do not mean he shares a responsibility or obligation for them. Medea did them freely out of love, and he does not bear responsibility for them;

D. *his actions benefit Medea, and she should be grateful*: he argues that he is being rational, thinking things through in a way that will benefit her and their entire family in the long run. Jason argues he is a friend to Medea. Jason reiterates how his actions benefit the standing of their family, it secures a place for them in Corinth, that she can be his mistress, and over time both families can unite (effectively with royal standing).

Does Medea's justifiable anger justify deceit? Does it justify the loss of lives, including her own children? It cannot. But affirming that Medea takes the gravely wrong path does not resolve the predicament. Jason's indifference to his evils and his unrepentance remains. It is his cowardice and indifference that drive Medea to such terrible lengths. Acknowledging that Medea has made the worst choices does not alleviate the difficulty of justice and forgiveness. Jason has thoroughly enclosed himself against the experience of genuine remorse. How is he to *learn* the injustice he has caused unless it does involve the glaring and messy business of life? Medea's revenge certainly wakes Jason up! Medea's terrible responses are uneasily effective in concretizing for Jason what he has done. With the death of his family and children he has now experienced the horror of what it means to lose one's family, to forsake one's bonds. Medea disabuses him of the belief that his owns sins leave him unscathed. How, then, do we proceed? How do we avoid the sinfulness of Medea's response but retain some form of its effectiveness? Don't we want to experience the awfulness of our sin rather than ignorantly believing it's a mere error? We often commit sins repeatedly because we do not feel the horror of our actions. If forgiveness is to be transformative, justice must also be. Justice must teach and transform hearts and minds toward the good.

How can justice walk that tightrope? In a fallen world it may be difficult, even impossible, to achieve such succinct moral calibration. Perhaps the best option is to turn the other cheek. But is turning the other cheek fraught with its own difficulties? Does this action allow justice to go on unchecked, or rather deferred as God's problem? Perhaps becoming the supreme problem. Is the Christian choice only *tacitly* recognizing the injustice? Is turning the other cheek an insufficient, mediocre, and anemic justice that weeps like a gaping wound badly bandaged? Will such a form of justice turn septic? Or is our turning of the cheek the most powerful form of resistance because it is the surrender to the divine form of justice?

The Impossible Possibility

Anger is a purifying emotion. It is the fundamental mechanism of morality which staves off apathy and indifference. It brings personhood out of an overly abstract and theoretical view of life. Morality is often derived from the social netting of how we feel about one another personally, politically, and religiously. Our status as moral persons rests on our ability to take a stance, to be affected, to be swept up and fight for perceived goods and against perceived evils. Morality is a tension between an intellectual understanding of the Good and a sentiment-based exercise. If morality is rooted in what we care about, then Medea's anger should be a guiding emotion, fighting off the dryness of intellectual indifference. Anger directed toward a particular situation and a perceived injustice has that power to arouse feelings, to change minds, to shame those who do evil. But if justice and mercy are *only* sentiments, rooted in personal or collective perceptions, then the need for salvation dries up. Forgiveness would be reduced to relativism. Each act of forgiveness would be ruled by opinions and perceptions, with its own rules, making hell on earth.

What is the universal good of forgiveness if only a psychological sentiment? Forgiveness cannot undo what has been done. If it is only a sentimental or psychological experience, then we cannot claim it to be a universal good at the core of human nature and experience. In such a lamentable scenario, each person would have to decide whether forgiveness is valuable, based on whether it will benefit his or her psychology. This applies to both the victim and the victimizer. Both would have to determine the condition and value of forgiveness before deciding what actions are deemed offensive or not, relative to each. Each may choose to support or reject this exchange on the basis of personal preferences at the time. This means that the question of actual guilt would not be central to the issue of forgiveness! The issue would be whether our giving or receiving of forgiveness (for whatever offense, whether it is an offense at all!) benefits us emotionally at that time and place. In a sentimentalizing view of forgiveness, demanding or giving forgiveness is indifferent to whether the act is truly sinful and whether it can wash away our sin. What becomes meaningful is whether the eloquent language of the pardoned and the pardoner accomplishes superiority among competing psychological perspectives.

What becomes of a world where forgiveness is reduced to a psychological mindset? What would be the point of forgiveness? Why all the rigmarole when there are a multitude of easier ways to experience euphoria, pleasure, peace, and release? Why deal with the sticky business of forgiveness at all?

Forgiveness must be more than a sentimentalizing addition. If not, "Thy will be done" becomes the motto not only of the atheist, but of the person who sees no reason to forgive or to be forgiven. "Forgive us our trespasses as we forgive those who trespass against us" would become tweaked based on the conditions of each historical era. The entirety of Medea's person is enveloped in anger. She descends into wells of sin, but what drives her is objective justice, not mere personal offense. The question of atonement is far more serious than one of competing emotional stances. Medea misses the mark in devastating fashion! But she *still* recognizes the mark must be somewhere. The line that divides good and evil, heaven and hell, is at stake for her, as it is for all of us. Anger is uneasily but fundamentally at the core of the human experience. We stand somewhere between mortal and immortal, with a foot simultaneously in both camps yet a stranger alienated from full admission to both. Earth is neither heaven nor hell but is formed of both camps. We travelers must find the clues to our home within its unified womb and tomb.

When one act of violence occurs, it threatens to set off a chain reaction of endless retaliatory violence and vengeance. Sacrifice is instituted by each civilization to break the perpetual historical cycle of violence and endless revenge. Revenge though is not solely retaliatory. It also seeks to reform/teach the offender justice through a sheer experience of *how* the original offense was unjust. Vengeance is the punishment designed to express how much human beings abhor violence! But once within vengeance the cycle cannot be broken without sacrifice, which unites enemies in a common cause. We seek a common enemy to be sacrificed, which alleviates anger, tension, and desire for vengeance. Just as Jason's evils prompted Medea's revenge, her acts of vengeance occasion his threat of violence. There is no stopping this cyclical pattern of anger. Anger is exorcized in revenge, re-inflamed by the offender now offended exorcizing his own anger in revenge!

> It belongs to human nature to hate those you have injured.
> —Tacitus, *Agricola*

This view of violence can never be local: persons will go against persons, families against families, towns against towns, gods against gods within a competing cycle. When violence is at the point of threatening existence on a larger scale, an unnerving sociological mechanism arises, the scapegoat mechanism. This communal violence is suddenly projected upon a single innocent individual or a separated and earmarked group. Persons and tribes that were formerly fighting and exacting vengeance on the other, now unite in an effort against a chosen individual or group as scapegoat. These enemies become alliances and even friends as they communally and ritually participate in the execution of violence against a common enemy. And this violence temporarily, for generations, stops. This cyclical avenging and violence, culminating in the powerful enjoining of enemies who become allies, allows civilization to flourish.

What then would be forgiveness but a companion to violence helping to govern and purge its baser instincts? We would not have any sense of forgiveness above a sociological framework. Forgiveness would not be in the image and likeness of the Christ Who seeks in His passion and resurrection the total transformation of each human person. Christ's sacrifice cleans the slate that condemned us to death. Opposed to Christ, that cycle of violence has anger and revenge as terminating in a sacrifice that is "redemptive." But only temporarily and loosely redemptive. That violent cycle must be played out, again and again, in all of existence. Any sense of forgiveness is nothing more than another term for the temporary alleviation of violence. This view of forgiveness is not truly transcendent, not full of grace. This is not the mercy offered by Christ on Good Friday. Nor is it the forgiveness that can separate the wheat from the chaff, the sheep from the goats, the heavenly from the hellish. Such a diminished notion of forgiveness is nothing other than violence instituting a temporary unity. The violence, separation, and revolt at one end of the pendulum, climaxes in its artificial opposite: sociological forgiveness as the time to remold society to its will. Sociological violence and forgiveness both serve the same purpose—the remolding of culture and values—and are only a difference of affectivity, and not in nature.

Medea's oppressive "redemptive" revenge cannot emancipate itself from this violent cycle. It functions only from within its bondage. She attempts to transport Jason within the sheer experience of his offense. Medea wants to make him undergo the injustice he caused her with exacting precision. In this cycle there is no power to transform. At best, violence will be managed until the next rupture of this constructed imitation of unity. For Medea, justice means having the offender experience the evils of the injustice as a way of education, and eliciting guilt. Because of this, Medea views the murder of her children as regrettable but necessary violence. This act of sheer incalculable violence alone is capable of breaking Jason, of destroying his core of indifference and shamelessness. But this so-called cyclical

FORGIVENESS

redemptive violence can never truly redeem the situation. She hesitates briefly before killing her children, calling her actions a "terrible but necessary wrong." In Medea, all things are bound to our fallenness. Goodness, redemption, and justice are wedded to evil, violence, and deceit such that none of these attributes is really the opposite of any other. In such a view, there can be no forgiveness beyond a sociological or pragmatic framework. There can be no heaven either. In the end it is indistinguishable from hell.

The gospel is the true alternative in the difficulty of forgiveness. It reflects the pinnacle of this cycle of anger and violence finally giving humans a way to avoid redemptive violence with redemptive suffering. Christ is the spotless victim. He is the holy innocent. As fully human and fully God, He is the highest victim of redemptive violence and the Being Who can overcome this cycle. His life, death, and resurrection break the cycle of redemptive violence with redemptive suffering. In the gospel, the church (Caiaphas) and state (Pilate) subversively unite and conspire to condemn Jesus; two enemies become allies. Christ becomes the ideal victim to exorcise the church and the state's guilt, to impart pseudo-redemption and sociologically rooted variations of forgiveness and harmony. But Jesus is no ordinary victim: "Father, forgive them, for they do not know what they do." Christ knows *exactly* why He is the supreme victim, and to what depths He must descend to break this terrible cycle that ends in death for all. When He offers us the gift of heaven within His flesh and blood, He offers us forgiveness in a manner immeasurably greater than any sociological modeling that roots forgiveness only in sentiment and not in salvation and truth. Christ's passion completes the highest act of redemptive violence. His resurrection overcomes that violence. Christ replaces violence with the gift of redemptive suffering which can *truly* forgive. He loved us before the foundation of the world!

> For you know that it was not with perishable things such as silver or gold that you were redeemed from the empty way of life you inherited from your forefathers, but with the precious blood of Christ, a lamb without blemish or spot. He was known before the foundation of the world, but was revealed in the last times for your sake. Through Him you believe in God, who raised Him from the dead and glorified Him; and so your faith and hope are in God.
> —1 Peter 1:18–22

Christ transforms that redemptive violence which temporarily sets things "straight" but inevitably returns us to emptiness and meaningless suffering.

He offers us redemptive suffering as a truer form of forgiveness, as passage to eternal life. Christ taught us how to transform ourselves, "to put off the old self" in ourselves. Rather than blame others, we are each sinners seeking Christ's mercy. If any person has a right to hold a grudge, it is Christ. He is wholly innocent, and offers only Goodness, Truth, and Beauty. Christ offers forgiveness with unending love to those incapable of achieving it on their own. We see genuine anger in Christ overturning the tables of the money lenders in the temple. There is no false tolerance within Him. There is nothing to muddy the water of His suffering and redemption. Nothing undervalues His forgiveness. Christ does not hold a grudge. If God, His Father, were to retain a justifiable vengeance toward us, then there would be no salvation. There would be no heaven, no love that outwits death. What then is the appropriate balance between anger as purgative, and forgiveness as release, that does not undervalue the delicate relationality of self and other? What type of forgiveness, genuinely, heartrendingly mindful of trespasses both enacted and underwent, leads us to heaven?

Why Should I Ask People to Forgive Me When I Commit Injustice?

> God, I have to wait. You make me wait long enough.
> You make me wait long enough for repentance after a fault
> And contrition after a sin,
> And since the beginning of Time I await
> Judgement until the Day of Judgement.
> —Charles Péguy, *The Mystery of the Holy Innocents*

What right do I have to request, let alone demand, forgiveness? What gives my faith the power to presume so much over another person? And to enable that presumption to go so far as to have God Himself wash our feet? I have trespassed in a such a way that what is lost cannot easily be recovered or recovered at all. Isn't it a form of injustice in asking to receive the very forgiveness of which I am wholly unworthy? By accepting forgiveness, am I shortening the experience of punishment and guilt needed to come to terms with my culpability? But then, is it not the nature of forgiveness to inhabit the lives of those unworthy to receive it?

The relationship between justice and forgiveness reflects one of the most pressing human situations: the notion of divine punishment in the afterlife. In our freely chosen actions, we have made ourselves unworthy. It is fitting that the hand of justice deal with us. But by making ourselves unworthy, we are in the very state that necessarily defines forgiveness, giving forgiveness its subject matter. What is forgiveness without those *unworthy* to receive it, who, through grace, can ask to be healed? "Lord, I am not worthy that you should enter under my roof, but only say the word and my soul shall be healed." Genuine forgiveness works from a different angle than authentic justice. At the same time, they are never incompatible in their goals for cultivating goodness, happiness, and redemption. Justice seeks to balance those precarious scales between innocence and guilt. On earth, this must be ceaselessly fine-tuned to be as good as possible. We never quite find the right calibration.

Earthly justice is, with Pope Benedict XVI "a ray of beauty that strikes us to the quick, that almost 'wounds' us, and that invites us to rise toward God." We are always east of Eden, and west of heaven. There is no time spent in jail that recovers the death of the person, that pays one's dues. Dues must be paid to secure that order that enables love to become commensurate with life and truth, not its enemy. Forgiveness, on the other hand, recognizes the incongruity at root in all things. It tries to balance the scales of loss and gain through a superabundance of love. All of us are sinners. We are all wholly in need of love as spiritual foundation. We cannot expect the grieved not to experience resentment for the victimizer who committed the injustice. But both the grieved and the victimizer, within the painful netting of original sin, have an obligation to restore the love, trust, and goodness that was wounded.

The trespasser audaciously reveals the universal obligation to acknowledge our original sin. We are each bound to other people. We have a responsibility to counteract every single sin, both our own and those of others. Each of us should desire to recover the love and good nature squandered at its root. No sin is in isolation, every act is within the fabric of our relationships. Each person is a self in relation to other people. There is no justice served in resentment. It is a worldly attempt to balance the scales through lack of love. We try to balance the scales of justice but flatten out the world into lovelessness. We surrender the heart of human longing and place ourselves in the earthly hell of alienation from God. Love that is salvific cannot coexist with resentment. All grief demands the impossible: the possibility of the beauty of forgiveness too magnificent to contain.

> Filled with rapture, his soul yearned for freedom, space, vastness.
> Over him the heavenly dome, full of quiet, shining stars, hung

> boundlessly. From the zenith to the horizon the still-dim Milky Way stretched its double strand. Night, fresh and quiet, almost unstirring, enveloped the Earth. The white towers and golden domes of the church gleamed in the sapphire sky. The luxuriant autumn flowers in the flowerbeds near the house had fallen asleep until morning. The silence of the Earth seemed to merge with the silence of the heavens, the mystery of the Earth to be touched by the mystery of the stars.... Alyosha stood gazing and suddenly, as if he had been cut down, he threw himself to the Earth.... It was as if threads from all those innumerable worlds of God all came together in his soul, and it was trembling all over, "touching other worlds." He wanted to forgive everyone for everything, and to ask forgiveness, oh, not for himself! but for all and for everything, "as others are asking for me," rang again in his soul.
> —Fyodor Dostoevsky, *The Brothers Karamazov*

Is My Forgiveness Unjust?

(Or, if a person is guilty, what is the point of forgiving that other? That person's guilt needs to be settled through his/her own actions not mine. Am I prematurely extinguishing the just experience of guilt in the one who is guilty?)

For the ancient Greeks, there is no forgiveness as it is crystallized in Christianity. Christian forgiveness forever changed human relationships. We may question whether that change benefits us. Does forgiveness usher in the putrefaction of all those passions that reflect genuine vitality? What level of commitment does the trespassed-against have in forgiveness? Is the victim's role too centralized, too overburdened, and distracting? Perhaps the guilty party be left to its own devices as a more effective form of educating the offender. Perhaps the pardoner diminishes the obligations of extolling justice on a societal level. One person forgives the guilty party indifferent to other victims also affected by the trespasser's actions. Is a singular act of forgiveness fair? Or does it sidestep the unrecovered time and life by undervaluing the incalculable difference between actions and words? Are we alleviating the guilt that alone has the power to chasten the heart and transform conscience? Dostoevsky was intimately acquainted with the armory of torments within the act of forgiveness:

> Listen! I took the case of children only to make my case clearer. Of the other tears of humanity with which the Earth is soaked

> from its crust to its center, I will say nothing. I have narrowed my subject on purpose. I am a bug, and I recognize in all humility that I cannot understand why the world is arranged as it is. . . . I want to see with my own eyes the hind lie down with the lion and the victim rise up and embrace his murderer. I want to be there when everyone suddenly understands what it has all been for. All the religions of the world are built on this longing, and I am a believer. But then there are the children, and what am I to do about them? . . . I understand, of course, what an upheaval of the universe it will be when everything in Heaven and Earth blends in one hymn of praise and everything that lives and has lived cries aloud: "Thou art just, O Lord, for Thy ways are revealed." When the mother embraces the fiend who threw her child to the dogs, and all three cry aloud with tears, "Thou art just, O Lord!" then, of course, the crown of knowledge will be reached, and all will be made clear.
> —Fyodor Dostoevsky, *The Brothers Karamazov*

Forgiveness places an undue societal burden on the victim. And it does not place nearly enough on the one who is guilty. Leaving the victimizer unforgiven may be more just since it acknowledges the permanence of the trespass, the heartrending lasting consequences of evil actions. It is astonishing that harmony in heaven would mean the mother and father embracing the child's torturer and murderer; that the child whose life was terribly cut short also embraces his killer; that they each cry aloud of the goodness and justice of the Lord. This harmony appears impossible on earth and inconceivable in heaven. There must be atonement for the death of the child. But what does atonement do? Hell does not rectify the difficulty. If the victimizer is sent to hell, how does this help the child maimed and murdered? How does the irretrievable loss of one soul in hell create harmony in heaven and recover what is lost in the victim? If there is a hell, then there are souls lost forever, which is a terrible, inconceivable burden. Every soul was once someone's child. We must forgive to save ourselves from the fires of hell but how can we forgive when it is so difficult a reality to achieve?

Forgiveness places an extra torment and burden on the victim. It demands the impossible: to forgive the unforgivable. The things most in need of forgiveness are unforgivable, unremittable, impossible. Let us not delude ourselves. An act of love, surrender, and pardon, one that can go the distance and not fall into failed love, necessitates Christ. And His *"My God, My God, why have You forsaken Me"* more truly recognized the impossibility.

Christ's last words reflect the blinding abandonment and forsakenness within the total risk of forgiveness and redemption. Christ knew our failed loves far better than we do. He knows how little we can bear, and Our Lord endures for us the incongruity, the failed returns, the broken hopes, the many pseudo-harmonies that all live within the difficulty of forgiveness.

Society expects that we forgive, as if it is an unqualified and universal good. Does this only promote inner resentment? We are tasked with absolving an injustice that cannot be undone—the rape has happened, the theft has occurred, the assault cannot be magically removed. We are always under existential danger in pardoning, especially because we are all sinners. We may place ourselves in an inauthentic position as usurping God's role. We may misconceive the situation, imagining that we can offer transcendence, offer something beyond mere words uttered by one fallen being to another.

> Then one of the seraphim flew to me, having in his hand a burning coal that he had taken with tongs from the altar. And he touched my mouth and said: "Behold, this has touched your lips; your guilt is taken away, and your sin atoned for."
> —Isaiah 6:6–8

There is something to forgiveness that is unseemly. Forgiveness is offered like water, donned as the frock in our nakedness, handed out as party gifts. We cannot touch the lips of the person and take the guilt away. We are never touched with such burning fire that our own guilt is not only extinguished but filled with an abundance of goodness. This is what the Greeks warn us against. This powerlessness within us to offer and receive such a rare and holy remission must be soberly acknowledged. The grace of forgiveness is repeatedly and illegitimately dressed up as a human power. When our true powerlessness is misconceived as power it takes from us the cardinal virtues (i.e., prudence, temperance, justice, and fortitude). We bypass the time-consuming process by which the virtues must situate themselves within us. Cardinal virtues are our orienting excellences. Let us examine briefly the role of each in our lives:

> a. *Prudence*: the ability to ascertain the correct course of action, the appropriate response for each situation. Prudence balances the longer way of a human life where universal truths must be accessed through daily experiences.

b. *Temperance*: This is a vigorous virtue. It is the humming, translucent, inviting soundness that can permanently unite the mind and body in the *same* desire. Its effects are moderation, restraint, and self-control, but its root is *eros* in its interplay with *agape*. Temperance recognizes that no earthly perfection is to be found, and that perfection is found only in the grace of heaven.

c. *Justice*: This virtue is the demand for fairness. It never confuses that with pseudo-equality or a forced uniformity of values. Justice is hierarchical, exhaustive, and places us in our relationship with the divine. Justice never falls into the trappings of relativism. It discovers fairness and truth through its intrinsic association with human nature as oriented toward the supernatural. Evidence of a corrupt society is the incessant changing of laws. This illustrates the lack of foundational justice. A society of pure opinions and sentiments can never rise to community because it is not united to transcendent human nature. The liar and the corrupt create the "ideal" state, conjuring a dream, a fantasy. This is the construction of a social contract over and against truth. Each member acts out the lowest common denominator of pleasures and whims, injustice itself. Injustice reduces categories such as truth, happiness, perfection, fulfillment, goodness, and beauty to opinion.

d. *Fortitude*: Fortitude gets us through the uneasy business of life. We are always skirting the edge of annihilation. This is the virtue that wears armor and a sword. It is the image of the crucifixion, it is the bearing of wounds, sweat, the protruding rib cage, the beginnings of putrefaction. This is the virtue that endures death, and it does so without denial, dismissal, false hope, nihilism, or scientism. Through fortitude we are freed to confront our human limitations and our need to offer up our lives to God. Fortitude bears the agonizing incongruity of human life. We are made for everlasting life but now must find it through suffering and death.

If forgiveness is authentic, it must be guided by these virtues, which set out the proper timeliness for every action, word, and deed. Forgiveness reveals in us the yearning for heaven. Through these directing virtues, forgiveness stretches across our bodies inhabiting even our fingertips, pointing to heaven. To pardon and be pardoned is the most serious affair in all of life. They foreshadow what it means to be forgiven by our Father through

Christ on the cross. Every failure of love resides within acts of forgiveness. Every dead end, every unresolved hope and dream exist either to be exorcised or transformed within this most impossible of acts.

The cardinal virtues show us the true approach to forgiveness where we undergo a lifetime of transcendent experience. The danger of forgiveness is that it often seeks to outwit this time-consuming process. Quick forgiveness seeks to settle and suppress the agony at root in the difficult business of sacred living. This well-meaning but empty forgiveness becomes the stumbling block of the virtues. It becomes the quick word and passing phrase in which we set aside the demands of our human responsibility in favor of caricatures of superficial tolerance and artificial kindness. Forgiveness is the chief blessing. It saves us. But it has a more popular doppelganger which is the porter at the gates of hell. While there is a temptation not to forgive, we may also counterintuitively say that there is a temptation to forgive thoughtlessly. We even become complicit in guilt through premature unexamined forgiveness. While we can more easily recognize the dangers of the refusal to forgive, let us not confuse thoughtless and premature forgiveness as mere error. If genuine forgiveness is a supreme blessing, then false, dishonest forgiveness is a grave predicament. It is the failure to be in the image and likeness of Christ, while acting to the contrary. To act as if the word "forgiveness" conjures the deed is the tyranny of the fool:

> Like a thorn that falls into the hand of a drunkard is a proverb in the mouth of a fool. Like an archer who wounds at random is he who hires a fool or passerby. As a dog returns to its vomit, as a fool repeats his folly.
> —Proverbs 26:9–11

When we misplace forgiveness and misuse it in situations that need more time and attention, we become disengaged from its genuine reality in our lives. Such questions as "how do we forgive or be forgiven for actions done out of ignorance?" and "how is forgiveness even possible if one party refuses entirely?" need to be given attention. Often in forgiveness, we ignore the arduous time-consuming way of the virtues and look for a quick fix. We are in danger of being unable to call to mind the genuine dimensions of forgiveness, of becoming simply unaccustomed to its presence.

How do I forgive if the person does not want to be forgiven, or if the person is dead? How do I receive forgiveness if it is denied to me, or if the person has died? Can we legitimately say forgiveness can easily occur in these accounts? Forgiveness is a relationship. These examples demonstrate that the relationship that would have enabled forgiveness has been removed. How do I forgive the one who killed the child, when I am not the child, not the one who died? Do I have that right? The deceased child who has that right has been stripped of that justice by the injustice of his death. Do I have the right to make that victim's choice? In these difficulties, we may condemn forgiveness to death, as we did when we crucified Christ. We repeatedly and practically kill off forgiveness in shallow tolerance and in the hostile demand for peace at all costs. Accept everything or die, forgive everything or perish, replace forgiveness with the denial of sin. The world has begun to deny sin. If this is the case, then there is nothing in need of forgiveness but the death of those still seeking forgiveness! This reality lines the very halls of academia.

> Finally, it is no longer completely fantastic to think that a day may come when not the executioners alone will deny the inalienable rights of men, but when even the victims will not be able to say why it is that they are suffering injustice.
> —Josef Pieper, *The Four Cardinal Virtues*

Perhaps Forgiveness Should Be Utilitarian?
(Or shouldn't forgiveness be utterly gratuitous, but then what does it add to the situation, if utterly gratuitous?)

What calculable gain do we get from forgiveness? Often, we "feel" better, we gain a sense of goodwill, an elation in overcoming such hurdles as anger and resentment. Perhaps being the pardoner evokes a sense of superiority. We gravitate toward that superiority a little too frequently. Sometimes forgiveness is a heady intoxicant. We are too ashamed to admit the baser motivations for forgiveness. Within us is a recognition that forgiveness provides a social advantage in future relations with the one we pardon. Through forgiveness we can do the very opposite of what it intends. We do not wash away the debt but make the pardoned the debtor in which no repayment is sufficient. In such a view, "you are forgiven and now you owe me" is the prevailing demand. And what is owed is an ever flexible and mercenary bounty. Counterfeit forgiveness trades in vitiated spirits and emotional enslavement. It is often strung out over years and decades. We recognize that these manipulative structures and various power plays, ever more intimate and deceitful, cannot be the true essence of forgiveness. But we are at a loss to its genuine nature. We have difficulty understanding how to utilize forgiveness authentically. We lose how forgiveness is an essential companion to the sanctifying and rigorous timing of the cardinal virtues. The pantomime of counterfeit forgiveness appears to function quite effectively. It functions in the absence of understanding what exactly forgiveness embodies. It works so well that we slip into its netting more easily each time we use it.

When we look at counterfeit forgiveness within the sphere of emotions and sociopolitical advantage, we are presented with two main outlooks:

> a. *Contractual Forgiveness*: forgiveness as a kind of contractual peacemaker, a checks-and-balances to quell social unrest. I forgive you. You forgive me. We do not look toward some perfect state, such as heaven. We keep each other in line by what we "owe" each other through giving and receiving pseudo-pardon.

This type of forgiveness involves the most minimal amount of moral and spiritual intention. Forgiveness, within reason, should be given as quickly as possible, deftly avoiding the minutiae that will lead nowhere but to dead-ends and anxiety. Forgiveness should not prompt those pesky spiritual questions that cannot be answered within materialism. The world is merely "out-there" and any sense of the experience of wonder is best to be ignored in favor of the pre-set, ready-made data we gather about the world. This especially includes how to navigate social situations through acceptable forms of pardon. This social contract of forgiveness should change its value in view of the cost-benefit ratio.

> There is one factor that undergirds every aspect of these apologies—it is fear, fear of the cultural power of the accusers, of their ability to ruin careers, reputations, and lives. These kinds of confessions aren't wrung from the accused under threat of torture or exile. But they are in some real sense coerced, which is why they ring so false and are so alarming in a free society.
> —Lowry, "The Humiliating Art of the Woke Apology"

Forgiveness should never stretch one beyond calculable gain. If pardoning is more worthwhile than not, then such a path should be traversed. If life is more robustly lived enjoying oneself and requesting forgiveness when needed, then this is the only sensible path. To do more would be absurd, out of character, and utterly out of bounds. Forgiveness cannot stretch us beyond ourselves. It must not demand too much. Contractual forgiveness cannot expect that our debtors should be released. This kind of forgiveness is unable to aim at a genuine resolution. It will not rectify an injustice. Nor will it make the guilty—to whom the pardoner may be closer in kind—any less culpable. Its refusal of any divine meaning prevents in advance any authentic existential resolution. In fact, it does not want these resolutions. At its core, contractual forgiveness functions within parasitical and predatory consciences. Despite all the efforts to manage, subdue, and indoctrinate reality, the world is full of surprise, chance, contingency, error, deficit, loss, inexplicable evil. This false forgiveness, which places a moratorium on genuine human relationship, sets us up for nihilism, which comes to roost at the inevitable moments of weakness, old age, and decline.

> It's obvious that the happy man feels contented only because the unhappy ones bear their burden without saying a word: if it weren't for their silence, happiness would be quite impossible. It's a kind of mass hypnosis. Someone ought to stand with a hammer at the door of every happy contented man, continually banging on it to remind him that there are unhappy people around and that however happy he may be at the time, sooner or later life will show him its claws and disaster will overtake him in the form of illness, poverty, bereavement and there will be no one to hear or see him.
> —Anton Chekhov, "Gooseberries"

Contractual forgiveness fails to direct us to heaven. A contract presupposes each can offer goods the other needs. We need the eternal life that Christ alone can offer us. But there is nothing we can give Him that He needs. He did not need the death, the suffering, the abandonment which we offered Him when He underwent the passion. Christ's passion is the last contract, which broke all contracts. Our Lord replaced contract with the covenant of superabundant love. This is love that forgives those unworthy of receiving it. Christ gave Himself neediness, hunger, pain, suffering, and death to break us from the cycle of our trespasses and defective forgiveness. Our forms of forgiveness are a series of failed transcendences ending in the many deadly forms of power and delusion which are but preludes to the dust and ashes.

> b. *Impertinent Forgiveness*: In this type of anti-forgiving, we ask ourselves why we should be obligated to another, either by the need to forgive or to be forgiven. This attitude revolts against the artificiality of contractual forgiveness. But it is susceptible to forming a new social contract of its own.

The Impossible Possibility

Impertinent forgiveness sees the baseness of contractual forgiveness. "*I forgive you, now you owe me, now you must forgive me, you hypocrite.*" Forgiveness needs to be a fully gratuitous act. The pardoned and pardoner repeatedly violate its authenticity through their mercenary exchange of goods, selling off pieces of the soul. The impertinent and anarchic see the folly of it all.

This person rebels at the spiritual bondage and enslavement of wills by the act of pseudo forgiveness, which claims to offer liberation. Why am I taking the other person so seriously that I am binding everything up in that viewpoint, in this action, or non-action? With Rand in *Atlas Shrugged*: "It is against the sin of forgiveness that I wanted to warn you. You had the greatest chance in life. What have you done with it?" You have wasted your life in a cycle of forgiveness that destroys vital passions and replaces them with enfeebled ineptitude. Such a view believes that we are stronger and healthier if we have the strength to shrug off all the insignificant trespasses. Why be bound up in the petty transgressions that preoccupy our time? Only the idiot, the insane, or the religious choose the road of turmoil and protracted forgiveness.

Forgiveness is viewed with indifference, and this is where its own bondage may take effect. The instinct of the impertinent is certainly correct: much of forgiveness is a forgery, a bondage rather than a loving compassionate linking. Pseudo-forgiveness involves egos being "wounded" and the incessant and whining resurrection of past anger and resentment. But an attitude that thinks it can stand above the fray creates spiritual homunculi. There are debts and debtors. We cannot place ourselves outside of our own debts or the debt of others, which are indelibly connected to us. Impertinent indifference may recognize hypocrisy, but itself is too powerless meaningfully to explore the difficulty of forgiveness. It is all too familiar with people infused with anger and vengeance. But itself has very little corrective mercy. When was the last time we let our souls be infused with trust, friendship, and fidelity with the same intensity we devote to anger? Forgiveness should be an exercise in cultivating magnanimity through justice with the same force with which we cultivate anger and the lust for vengeance. Being aloof to our situation and our need for forgiveness only further attaches itself to the debts we owe. Impertinence surrenders itself to ignorance through a Titanomachy of self-enclosed egos. Each indifferent ego is unable to get outside the loop. We know ourselves only in relation to other people where we learn shared joy, suffering, and forgiveness.

Difficulties thus far: it seems that for forgiveness to be meaningful something must truly benefit both parties, or all parties involved. It also seems that for forgiveness to be central to human meaning and existence, it must be *more* than a psychological changing of sentiment, which would remain conditional and not a universal good. It also appears that forgiveness actually has to change what looks to be set in stone and unable to be changed, which renders genuine forgiveness salvific but exotic and rare. Forgiveness, which is transformative and thus more than changing emotive sentiments, necessitates that something divine must be intermingled with human life, that heaven has dwelt on earth, and we cannot escape its promise. We recognize our powerlessness to undo or change the past, we cannot slow aging, we cannot stop death, we cannot undo a choice we made. Where then shall we find forgiveness? How and where are the unforgiven redeemed?

2

The Unknowing Heart of Forgiveness

THE PROBLEM OF HELL

Luminous Mysteries, **by Carol Scott**

The Unknowing Heart of Forgiveness

Today I was late, a poor soul lost in the depths, young man not thirty
Jumped on the track, what else but oblivion
There is no sweetness, he waded out into the shallows and sunk
No water to float, what else but fallen
How did he decide the moment before, the hour, the day, always the day
If only there was a way to lure back time, wade back, back in line
Back to home and to life
His mother out of place, somewhere in the inner space
The outer spaces, the heart cannot break, it simply implodes, sunken stone
The earth's loneliest passage, only heaven knows
Was there nothing left, no creation to tread, no laughter, no broken bread
Nothing to stave off death
Did he know love, the close under closeness, the candlelight, moonlight, all
    lights
Did he know comfort, a home to himself
The inhaled scented bed, clean and fresh, the dizzy hint of new day
Was there no lover, no peace, no child, no half-glanced bliss
Unknown life, once in a lifetime life, never again life, mangled bruised
    broken life
The house of eternal life, ripped from its sockets life, the marrow below life
This life, forgive us God, forgotten now for we are late
It is getting late, the train and bus and trains again, all to circumnavigate
    the death
What if I were motionless in the middle of steel, half a body, departed soul
Blood on the tracks, vortex of lack, slack jaw nothing, what if I was the
    dying?
If only I could lure back time, half a line, who can pay the heavy fine
The heart caves in, yelping bellowing grief, it cannot lick its wounds
Too entrenched, bleeding too furiously, mounting chasms of pain
The blood loss, the lost Son once an infant small as two hands
Promises sunk as stone, too far to catch again
God there needs to be a God to atone for this loss, dropped stone, wishing
    well of sin
God there needs to be a God, bring the Son home
Forgive us God, this life, forgotten now, it is getting late
    —"Today I Was Late" by Caitlin Smith Gilson

The Impossible Possibility

IN THE UNKNOWING HEART of forgiveness, the love needed to conquer all requires the remission of the irremissible past. Through it all, we do *and* do not know what we have done. Forgiveness appears too high a price to pay, too good a gift to receive, too impossible to accomplish. But if it were possible, it would grant us the soul truly ready for paradise. Real forgiveness requires the cancellation of a permanent unchanged past. The goal of forgiveness is to reach into locked history to heal and correct what has transpired. Forgiveness needs to debride the evil from the event. It needs to remove the harm that is woven inextricably into the fabric of the past and informing the present. The problem is that forgiveness appears an impossible goal, even for God. Reality has rules and what is real cannot be suspended, removed, undone. Certainly, God desires to help us, but how can He correct the course? Isn't what is done *already* finished? Forgiveness as remission, not mere sentiment, is the prerequisite for admission into paradise. But its actual occurrence appears impossible, even for God. This is an astonishing predicament!

How does God's justice and mercy unify genuinely and not problematically? The question of heaven is also the dilemma of hell. On one end we understand that God sending His only Son reaffirms the divine desire that all persons be saved. God wills only salvation for us. He does not will that we should go to hell. This is wholly contrary to divine love. Hell is permanent abandonment from God. It evokes pain and suffering beyond all imagining, forever alienated from creation, the Creator, and love. Such a reality is wholly at odds with Christ's desire to save all sinners. It seems wholly opposed to God's mercy.

Hell realizes a state wherein the work of mortal man can undo the work of divine salvation! Yes, God does not send us to hell. Instead, we freely refuse the call. Presented with the promise of infinite love and mercy, and for reasons strange and heartbreaking, we can freely reject that eternally beautiful courtship. Does God truly surrender His will by allowing our wills to forfeit His power, *against* our own good, and with devastating results? This presents more than a conundrum in terms of God's divine goodness. It presents a moral and spiritual reckoning itself.

To deny universal salvation and affirm that some persons indeed are irredeemably separated from God may devalue Christ's total desire for the salvation for all. It may also diminish His supreme power to save and undermine the worthiness of His ultimate sacrifice. It also seems to place too heavy a price to pay on finite creatures, who "know not what they have done." To affirm universal salvation may devalue our gift of image and likeness to God Who gives us free will to act in His image. Our free will is the prime gift needed for love and redemption in the first place. Our *imago Dei* means that we are responsible for our choices and for the good and evil they bring. We must accept that we live or die by those consequences. Otherwise, we forfeit our very nature as spiritual beings. We are, for St. Thomas Aquinas, far closer to the angels than the animals. We have the power to make hell for ourselves by repeatedly refusing God's call. If we demonstrate that we do not want God by refusing Him repeatedly, why would it be fair for God to force our hand? Hell is the place for those who do not want God's love. Why would it be just for God to force those persons into salvation? And if forced, then we are not in heaven at all! Salvation is the only ultimate good for us, but a forced nuptial invalidates that good.

In Favor of Universal Salvation

We pray for all people to be saved. Shouldn't we trust in God's will over our own powers? Shouldn't we believe that God's desire for our salvation is stronger than the power of death, and of all human evils put together? Isn't this the inner dynamite of Easter Sunday? Christ descends into hell to break us free and save all mankind. Christ died for all sinners. He broke open the gates of hell. Are we to accept that His saving love cannot save all sinners? Are we to concede that the power of hell, and our own foolish choices, are stronger than He is? Such a belief is practically impossible. Again, would an all-powerful God really let the sinful works of mankind thwart His divine salvation? "Father, forgive them; for they know not what they do." Truly the more we enter sin, the less we are able to *see* and *experience* the horror of our sinfulness. That is why Christ, the spotless lamb and wholly innocent victim, suffers more than any other human being. He *knows* what we have done. The more we enter sin, the less free we are to be able to excise ourselves from its lies. There is something just and merciful about universal salvation, given how sin itself cripples us. Isn't Christ's justice supremely merciful? Whoever is without sin throws the first stone. He alone can throw that decisive stone, and He declined.

We are finite beings with limited understanding of the consequences of our actions. How is *eternal* damnation just when we live wholly within finite and limited knowledge? How is it the proportionate response to our finite human nature? Wouldn't it make more sense if the fires of hell are a sort of self-induced punishment? We place this punishment upon ourselves by our choices and it extends into the fires of the afterlife? What is first experienced as burning and turmoil, later warms and draws the person desirous of God. The difference between fire as hell and fire as beckoning salvation is the human response. These fires are themselves cleansing. They are wholly identical with God's infinite love. In universal salvation, even the most wicked sinner will recover the good that was once his and enter the warm light of salvation. Christ suffers most particularly for the unpardoned, for the great sinner. None of us has ever loved God with all our heart. None of us has ever loved God with our whole soul. None has loved God with complete passion, ardor, and strength. We are all unworthy for Him to enter under our roof.

Acknowledging the Real Possibility of Hell

It may not be unjust to pray for all to be saved, but isn't it unjust to believe all are saved? What is the point of confession, of forgiveness for our sins, of avoiding temptation and sin, of the liturgy, if *all* are saved? If all are saved, then the hedonist is the best utilitarian! The hedonist is taking the only sensible line: pleasure here on earth, and the certain expectation of pleasure in the afterlife. Why cover the tabernacles on Good Friday? Why claim that Christ truly dies every Good Friday, of every year, of every century, if sins by our own obstinate choices do not have the power to "uncrown a hope in God"? If sin is not irremediable and irredeemable then Christ did not need to embark on the rescue mission. Is restoration to the origin and recovery of what is lost truly possible? It cannot be a just and good act if it violates our free will. Our freedom enables us to choose our path in life, realize what kind of person we are, and even to refuse divine love.

There has never been 100 percent clarity in knowing what will happen to us and others by the choices we make, both good and bad. But we are responsible to follow the good, whatever the results. In our sinful actions, we are never in a position fully to know the panorama of outcome. We do not know fully what will happen if we lie, or cheat, or steal, or murder, but we *know* they are wrong, that they are shortcuts. We recognize these sins in our conscience. It is not necessary to know completely what consequences occur because of our actions in order to decide whether or not to act. No human has ever been given this amount of knowledge. We are not Prometheus, but we are still responsible. Even Prometheus' foreknowledge did not give him fore-experience. He knew what would happen, that he would be betrayed, but he did not know how it would feel, the pain and anguish took him by surprise. Even Prometheus did not conquer the full panoply of consequences, but this does not invalidate his responsibility. It is not ours to decide who goes to heaven and who goes to hell. It is not ours to say that God's mercy wipes away hell. Nor is it ours to say that hope for universal salvation is off the table. Least of all, it is not ours to claim that our sins are finite. When we commit murder, we know the victim has lost his earthly life forever. We kill the most innocent in the womb. We know we are extinguishing the long and meandering realm of possibilities and generations that rightfully belong to the unborn. We understand that we irrevocably alter the lives of many beyond the immediate victims of our transgressions. Why can't we freely refuse God's grace with the same permanence? Why can't we choose to send ourselves to hell?

> The entrance seemed to be by a long narrow pass, like a furnace, very low, dark, and close. The ground seemed to be saturated with water, mere mud, exceedingly foul, sending forth pestilential odors, and covered with loathsome vermin. At the end was a hollow place in the wall, like a closet, and in that I saw myself confined. . . . I felt a fire in my soul. . . . My bodily sufferings were unendurable. I have undergone most painful sufferings in this life . . . yet all these were as nothing in comparison with what I felt then, especially when I saw that there would be no intermission, nor any end to them. . . . I did not see who it was that tormented me, but I felt myself on fire, and torn to pieces, as it seemed to me; and I repeat it, this inward fire and despair are the greatest torments of all. . . . I could neither sit nor lie down: there was no room. I was placed as it were in a hole in the wall; and those walls, terrible to look on of themselves, hemmed me in on every side. I could not breathe. There was no light, but all was thick darkness. . . . I was so terrified by that vision—and that terror is on me even now while I am writing—that though it took place nearly six years ago, the natural warmth of my body is chilled by fear even now when I think of it. . . . It was that vision that filled me with the very great distress which I feel at the sight of so many lost souls . . . for they were once members of the Church by baptism—and also gave me the most vehement desires for the Salvation of souls; for certainly I believe that, to save even one from those overwhelming torments, I would most willingly endure many deaths.
> —St. Teresa of Ávila

The Impossible Possibility

Isn't there a problem confusing the fires of hell with those of purgatory? This issue points not only to an error in judgment, but potentially unfastens the very connective tissue of human responsibility. If God extends His freeing image to us, we may use it for *this* or *that* choice, but these choices do over time reflect *how* we desire to be judged in light of the ultimate end. God makes the eternal choice to give humans free will. Our free choices always act themselves out within situations that have a view toward the ultimate. What major I choose, for example, is still pointing toward what role in life will fulfill me. Situational choices are always toward an end, a goal, an ultimate. Why would God suddenly treat His decision as conditional, finite, and limited, by conflating the fires of hell with the cleansing fires of purgatory? No situation is truly finite. No situation exists within a vacuum of pure environment. The finite indelibly points to the infinite, as human yearning pants for the divine. Without an "end" you might have environment, but you could not have a situation, which all moral quandaries are. The questions *what shall I do?* and *why shall I do it here and now?* both point toward an end. It is true that all ethical acts and decisions are situational. This is precisely because they *always* involve a relation to an end. A situation is a particular matrix of actuality and possibilities. Their order and meaning can only be determined in relation to the end willed or recognized. By its very nature, a situation refers beyond itself to a possible end. In other words, there is no such thing as an absolute situation except in relation to an absolute end. The "human condition" taken as a universal situation would be such an absolute situation. The very idea of an absolute, supreme, final, perfect, and complete end already involves the notion of situation. The situation helps us realize, approximate, and actualize the chosen end in ethical action.

The relationship of mercy and justice is not evidence of a disjointed caricature of God, a balancing juggler tossing too many unwieldy plates in the air. God is identical with love and offers only heaven. Then thumb a few pages down in the Gospels and it is better for Judas, and the many who are left outside the banquet, never to have been born. They are not even to be recognized by Christ when they knock feverishly at the door. Perhaps we reconcile these difficulties of forgiveness and harmony by problematically putting God in the same boat as ourselves. Perhaps we claim original sin inflicts a weakness on God, which, like us, He cannot overcome its irremediable consequences. Or to overcome it would be to commit a theological oxymoron—a merciful injustice. He cannot forgive us without undermining justice, rendering forgiveness unworthy *because* it is unjust. On the other hand, God must offer forgiveness, for without it, justice has no end or fulfillment, no transcendent purpose. If God *does not* forgive the obstinate sinner, then He is sending His own creature to hell where justice appears opposed to love. If God *does* forgive the obstinate sinner, He sends His creature to heaven against the creature's will, where love opposes justice. It appears to be a "damned if you do, damned if you don't" situation. What is to be done? Forgiveness without justice is meaningless, and justice without forgiveness annihilates human and divine relationships. God Who *is* Justice and Love does nothing to contradict Himself. Our goodness is enacted in freedom. If any of God's acts oppose that freedom, He would be opposing the very good of His creation united to Him. God, Who is perfect and all good, cannot oppose Himself. Does God fail in goodness by not saving us? But how does God avoid opposing His goodness if His salvation surpasses our free will? God's saving us against our will would violate our creation, and thus necessitates an impossible violation of God's perfection.

Is God Weak?

Have the consequences of our original sin affected God's ability to relate to us and save us? It was fitting to extend salvation through His only Son. But still, this doesn't mean we choose Christ. And in that situation, what does God do? Perhaps, God remains as distant degrees of love and justice through a metaphysical weakness of His Being. Original sin rendered God the inactive watchfulness of the referee. But is the weak God better than the non-existent God? The non-existent God does not give us false hope, and nothing is quite as vicious as hope that has no ability to be fulfilled. Such a God would be the diminishing of heaven into an old wives' tale, and then sheer irrelevance, and then finally to non-existence. Is this the reality of the situation we are in? It appears almost impossible to conceive of heaven as anything other than the naive celebration. Our difficulty may be a symptom of our very weak God. Is God so weak and His hands tied that there is no difference between His existence and non-existence, between heaven and no heaven at all? In grief, the hope for heaven is the promise of richness transforming the vacant lot. But we cannot quite envision the color, texture, and richness, only the vacant lot stares blankly back. We brush it aside, saying with half terror and half denial, *"never mind, it is the better place I do not yet know."* We do not know whether that is an act of faith or an act

The Impossible Possibility

of resignation from a congestive and failing faith. Besides, we will never be able to tell the difference, for God, in such a view above, is far too weak to guide us.

If God is going to intercede in raising our forgiveness from good intention, which is powerless to transform, to genuine transformative reality, everything discussed above are the stumbling blocks. These are the potholes along the road to Emmaus, and further on to our home in heaven. God does not violate our free will. We know this from the very drama of Christ's death and resurrection. Faith is not magic, and God's actions do not sidestep our free choice. We must wonder about the perilous journey when our freedom that God will not violate becomes the freedom for eternal death. Who can overcome all of this? Who can authentically enable this impossible harmony? We turn to the Gospels, to what may be the resolution. The passage is enigmatic and often eludes understanding: *"Father, forgive them, for they know not what they do."*

Can the expectation of forgiveness be reasonably sought if we do not know what we do? Christ can intercede on our behalf because we do not know what we do. The fallen angels knew entirely, that is why their damnation was complete and irrevocable. But if we do not know what we do, does this mean that we are less culpable? Strangely enough, does it mean we are less in need of forgiveness? This does not seem to strike us quite right. But let us follow the path into its painful bewilderment.

> Whether or not we are able to forgive: How can one forgive them at all, if they know not what they do! One has nothing whatever to forgive. But does a man ever know completely what he does? And if this must at least remain questionable, then men never do have anything to forgive one another and pardoning is to the most rational man a thing impossible. Finally: if the ill-doers really did know what they did—we would have the right to forgive them only if we had the right to accuse and punish them. But this we do not have.
> —Friedrich Nietzsche, *Human All Too Human*

Nietzsche's Rejection of Christian Forgiveness

Don't all sinful and evil acts revolve around ignorance and involve acting against our own best interest? In essence, why would anyone continue his present course when he has a better, more advantageous option in front of him? This ignorance seems naturally to occur because we do not grasp all the potential consequences of our choices. Unlike the angels, human beings appear handicapped from the start. We are responsible, though unable to know all the outcomes when deliberating potential choices. This handicap is sometimes dispelled in repeated actions, and in the cultivation of virtues. But often it is magnified and becomes the occasion for a thorough steeping in pride and sinfulness. There is no expectation given our limited knowledge that this blindness will be overcome. The natural world is full of contingency, risk, and chance. If guilt requires truly knowing that we did wrong, and knowing why we acted against our true self-interest, why would anyone do wrong? That is part of the mystery of Satan's fall, and this is why Nietzsche's understanding of forgiveness does not capture lived reality. Forgiveness in his view necessitates a more complete understanding of actions, events, situatedness, a self-knowledge above and beyond what humans possess. Christianity is, for Nietzsche, parasitical because it expects too much of us. It demands that we enact depths of pity and excessive humility to place ourselves into the orbit of forgiveness. And forgiveness is inaccessible to us.

The pardoned/pardoner structure is vampiric, for Nietzsche, and creates the pessimistic world that is against life. The demand for forgiveness is an enemy against vitality, fortitude, strength, and magnanimity. The pardoned and the pardoner cannot exist as two separate people with separate realities. Each is bonded to the other and to their failings. To forgive and be forgiven should instead exist as powers of the self. We are strong enough to understand the joy of nothing other than the force of our own decision. The higher, stronger person, for Nietzsche, is full of the will to power. He or she is magnanimous, fair, generous, benevolent. When the pardoner and the pardoned are realized as the same person, those strong passions are the natural reality. They are not insipidly forced upon us through shame, pity, and fallenness, the weapons of parasitical forgiveness. Nietzsche rejects our numbing effort to raise up what is nebulous, forgiveness, forcing it to become the good of nature and society. For Nietzsche, we must not allow the ill-constituted to define what is beautiful and healthy. Through an incessant and eroding cycle of forgiveness, we place ourselves at the mercy of the other. This is how we become infected with their pallid spiritual outlook. Then the beauty of *this* life is denied in favor of an afterlife unworthy of belief. For Nietzsche, Christianity's search for heaven is rooted in our refusal to live authentically within the world. Paradise, a world of irrational and impossible perfection, is as empty and meaningless as a side-less square. It is a result of a pity that holds us hostage to others. This kind of parasitical pity inverts the natural order and denies the strength of life. We do not know what forgiveness is because there is nothing deep to know about it. For Nietzsche, it is most assuredly a power-play, a maneuvering, and the most loathsome of the Christian deceits. The only way to conquer it is not to be held hostage to its promises of the afterlife.

"*Father forgive them, they know not what they do*" is, for Nietzsche, the primal contradiction that has malformed two thousand years of human progress. If we do not know what we do, if we do not have this complete knowledge, we are *not* in need of forgiveness. We are only in need of ridding ourselves of its yoke. Then, and only then, can we return to the powers that we do know, and to the goods that are their natural vital effects.

A Christian Response to Nietzsche

Why would anyone want to subscribe to Nietzsche's eerily prophetic teaching? How is life capable of any transcendence if forgiveness is only an unexperienced presupposition? Is forgiveness merely a theoretical reality experienced only by way of defection and bondage? If Nietzsche rejects the forgiveness that transforms souls and through God involves a cancellation of the sin, what remains? It appears to degrade itself into cheap sentiment. Nor does it escape the power-plays. But at least Nietzsche's view recognizes the sheer *difficulty* of forgiveness. He acknowledges the obscurity we should force ourselves to encounter when confronted with what it means to wipe away sin, and what it entails to give and receive pardon.

As a young man on pilgrimage in Mount Athos, the playwright Eugene Ionesco experienced the galling, unremitting mystery face to face. This event profoundly affected him and remained a cornerstone of Christian meaning and purpose for the rest of his life.

> I was born in an Orthodox family, and I lived in Paris. At twenty-five years, I was a genuine young man of the secular culture of the then Paris. I got the idea to visit Mount Athos because of its position as a place of asceticism in the Orthodox Church. And there I had another thought in mind: to confess. So I went and found a hieromonk, a spiritual father. What did I say to him? The usual sins of a secular young man who lives without knowing God. The hieromonk, after hearing me, said:
> "Do you believe in Christ my child?"

> "Yes, yes, I believe Father. Besides, I am baptized Orthodox Christian."
>
> "Well, my child, do you believe and accept fully that Christ is God and Creator of the world and us?"
>
> I lost it, because this was the first time a person put forward this question to me, and which I had to answer honestly and take a position. Not just if I believe someone made the world, but that this God, the Creator of the world, has to do with me. And that I have a personal relationship with him! I replied:
>
> "Father, I believe, but help me understand this fact well."
>
> "If you really believe, then all corrects itself."
>
> —Eugene Ionesco, *Paris-Match*

"If you really believe, then all corrects itself": this is the astonishing foundation in which we unite in the image of Christ. This is where our always failing words—to forgive and to be forgiven—do not dissipate but are raised into the architecture of heaven. It is inconceivable that God becomes a man Who exists *for us*. Our forgiveness seeks always to be infinite and everlasting. Forgiveness seeks to be the gatekeeper of every nuance that can possibly undo what cannot be undone. Forgiveness has always lived in the impossible territory of that which cannot be undone. It is always before us, and after us. It is in our midst as we walk, and into us in the grave, growing into our flesh, eluding our grasp. Our forgiveness yearns for heaven because a glimpse of heaven became incarnate on earth when God became human. Our forgiveness cannot be all these things. It cannot know fully what we have lost and gained in the giving, receiving, and refusal to give and to receive forgiveness. And yet it is and retains these things. Mercy is the apex in which we extinguish and resurrect all life and hope within us. Forgiveness is the altar at which we fumble, attempting to make ourselves an offering for the other and receiving more than we are in return.

> If you have faith as small as a mustard seed, you can say to this mountain, "Move from here to there," and it will move. Nothing will be impossible for you.
> —Matthew 17:20

Father, forgive them they know not what they do. Christ completes the sacrifice required in forgiveness, which we know but do not know, which we know by our failure to move the mountain. We know it in every recited prayer that contains within it the eternal Word united with our spoken word. We repeat the prayers our Father gave us, often with little passion, with little belief, and yet still, through the centuries, it is plenitude. We know the power of forgiveness in the failure of our words and deeds. Forgiveness is the prayer that contains the whole power of God as person Whose love became sacrificial, offering us the form of remittance that is transformative and real. Within the wounds of Christ, we reveal the one Word Who can offer and receive forgiveness as sins remitted, as saving and everlasting.

3

Three Mistaken Views on the Impossibility of Forgiveness

The Muses, by Carol Scott

The Impossible Possibility

I love you with the kind of mad love that unites the living and the dead
Understand, I would turn the world upside down
To tell you the things I cannot know

To the One Whom I Desire . . .

For all His gentleness and humility born flesh and blood
He descended as Star hurling through the cosmos
Stretched out Corpus Christi, knotted wood of my sighing

To My One Heart-Splitting All . . .

It is a terrible power to destroy love, this is the Sin before any one evil
The mystery of the gulf laced on lips, wreckages we cannot find
Misplaced life, dying time, death of our bodies, death of our kind

To My Body Towed through Weeping Glass for You . . .

We are fixed to die burning away
Hidden one we played the universe holding all the cards and lost

I love you with the kind of mad love that unites the living and the dead,
 understand I would turn the world upside down to tell you the things I
 cannot know

To My Hidden Lover Eclipsing Me Eden of Lapped Citrus and Wildflowers . . .

Hell is no place, but it is time, unrealized without His death, illusion in our
 power
The more as the lesser, fossil of the living

To You the Undressed Contours of My Mind . . .

What I do know is that if we lose out in every sense of the word, we are no
 longer persons
Persons make places, you make places, I think of your home, your home
To be home with you, loving you
But Hell is the loss of place, the more in Hell every love erased

   —"The Metaphysics of Love" (excerpt) by Caitlin Smith Gilson

Mistaken Views on the Impossibility of Forgiveness

We are born and often die unhappy. The most essential things in existence are often impossible. To shortchange this reality, to place the transformative demands of forgiveness within our own natural capacity, is a particularly cruel arrogance. It expeditiously renders forgiveness too possible for its own good. When forgiveness is too easily won, too much a given, the very netting of our transcendent experience of our own unworthiness, necessarily at root in grace, is squandered almost to its core. This all-too-common view makes heaven the scrap heap for any uneasy views of forgiveness that do not fit the equation. We must avoid serious reflection at all costs! Here, the desire for heaven is dramatically undercut, marginalized, and infantilized. Earthly norms have sufficiently psychologized forgiveness. What is left over, those set-aside dissatisfactions, have been stripped of any guidance. They are merely non-conformities, insignificant blips with no power to challenge the progressive therapeutic culture.

> Our Father, Who art in heaven, hallowed be Thy name; Thy kingdom come; Thy will be done on Earth as it is in heaven. Give us this day our daily bread; and forgive us our trespasses as we forgive those who trespass against us; and lead us not into temptation but deliver us from evil. For the kingdom and the power and the glory are yours forever.
> —Matthew 6:9–13

When forgiveness is viewed as achievable, utterly separate from the will of God, we make ourselves foolish God-usurpers, tin-pot dictators. When we lose the grace of "Thy will be done" we ignorantly separate forgiveness from the necessity for the remittance of sins. We reduce forgiveness to endless artifices of hurt, competing personal perspectives, and therapeutic remedies that are the earthly reactions when faced with the impossibility of forgiveness. None of these has the power to approach the demands of human-and-divine forgiveness.

On the other hand, those who recognize and resignedly accept the genuine impossibility of forgiveness are also susceptible to misunderstanding its power. We must avoid viewing the impossibility of the remittance of sins as disengaged from the blood of the Lamb. Christ washes white our baptismal robes with the most crimson of blood. The heart-aching impossibility to achieve genuine forgiveness within our own natural powers finds itself devolved into the following three alternatives, each failing fully to encounter the role of sacrifice. Each emphasize the impossibility of forgiveness while neglecting that *"with man this is impossible, but with God all things are possible"* (Matt 19:26).

The Promethean Heart

> Behold with what indignities mangled I shall have to wrestle through time of years innumerable. Such an ignominious bondage hath the new ruler of the immortals devised against me. Alas! alas! I sigh over the present suffering, and that which is coming on. How, where must a termination of these toils arise? And yet what is it I am saying? I know beforehand all futurity exactly, and no suffering will come upon me unlooked-for.
> —Aeschylus, *Prometheus Bound*

Here belong the hearts who have collapsed theory and practice, foreknowledge and fore-experience, knowledge and wisdom. They have the words but not the way. In losing the way, they find themselves startled and dismayed by the unseemly reality that reality and experience always exceed knowledge. This truth may not be fully understood by us until more is revealed and experienced. Forgiveness takes far more than knowledge and it takes far more than feeling. These hearts recognize that we need what we do not know how to grasp. They have discovered the gaping chasm that separates knowledge and wisdom. But they do not know how to traverse it. They give up in resignation and cannot encounter forgiveness as true remittance of sins, as an overcoming of the world. The Promethean Heart sees far ahead but never sees far enough. It refuses to surrender its own reason and trust in Christ Who alone enters under our roof.

> O world of spring and autumn, birth and dying
> The endless cycle of idea and action,
> Endless invention, endless experiment,
> Brings knowledge of motion, but not of stillness;
> Knowledge of speech, but not of silence;
> Knowledge of words, and ignorance of the Word.
> All our knowledge brings us nearer to our ignorance,
> All our ignorance brings us nearer to death,
> But nearness to death no nearer to GOD.
> Where is the Life we have lost in living?
> Where is the wisdom we have lost in knowledge?
> Where is the knowledge we have lost in information?
> The cycles of Heaven in twenty centuries
> Bring us farther from GOD and nearer to the Dust.
> —T. S. Eliot, *Choruses from the Rock*

The Tragic Heart

The Tragic Heart recognizes the tension between fate and free will. This person knows that even with many things beyond our control, nothing alleviates human responsibility. Nothing can emancipate us from the inescapable need to forgive and to be forgiven. We are faced with our choices and our responsibilities. Then this Heart is faced with the impossibility to make forgiveness what it needs to be—something more than psychological perspective, more even than the sinner suffering in grief and repentance.

> My shame and guilt confounds me.
> Forgive me, Valentine: if hearty sorrow
> Be a sufficient ransom for offence,
> I tender 't here; I do as truly suffer
> As e'er I did commit.
> —Shakespeare, *Two Men from Verona*

For the Tragic Heart, the whole of existence is often experienced in one event. It is as if universal time is caught up in a powerful moment. It appears as if this Heart is freed into harmony, and a forgiveness that can truly liberate us. But the experience becomes like the tablecloth pulled quickly beneath the plates. Everything is intact, everything still as it was, and nothing ultimately transformed. The Tragic Heart glimpses in forgiveness what could be, but more still experiences our tragic failure to undo what has been done. We experience life by way of our limitations and path in life. The All is only glimpsed. The Tragic Heart is liberated into that knowledge of the All and then trapped in its fate. We cannot complete the task at hand, we are left stranded and nomadic. We are fully responsible and yet unable to break free from the web of fate. We cannot wipe away sin, undo the past. The Tragic Heart has a transcendent moment in forgiveness where it experiences the All but cannot act upon it. This is the recognition of the necessity and impossibility of forgiveness, revealing the tragic essence in the heart of all of us. The Tragic Heart cannot move on. It fails to trust Christ and the heaven made through Christ, who alone fills us up, and fills us with the body of forgiveness.

The Heart (In)Justice

This is the Heart that recognizes the strange paradox of justifiable anger having little justifiable outlet. A parent's pure inconsolable anger in response to the murder of her child is justifiable, but then, the anger cannot act. It must exorcise itself into other forms in the name of measured justice. The parents must accept that the killer's legal punishment is, more often than not, *not* commensurate with the magnitude of the crime. A more commensurate retribution is paradoxically viewed as injustice. And even if the life of the killer is to be taken in return, this still is not commensurate. It fails to recover what is lost and buried, only adding another lost soul to the process. How odd is it that something such as justifiable anger cannot be acted upon easily? If it is a natural response, why doesn't it have an outlet? Where is the end that appropriately fulfills that anger, that authentically transforms it? We must take more than a moment to wrap our minds around earthly law. It is an essential structure of society. But it must perpetuate an imperfect sense of justice to enable civilization to function. The Heart (In)Justice recognizes how forgiveness attempts to fill the gap. Forgiveness seeks to rectify the incommensurate relationship between justifiable anger and earthly justice. Earthly forgiveness tries and fails to resituate justifiable anger beyond the reach of frustrated ends. Our earthly forgiveness attempts to orbit an end that can make sense of all the good and evil within the world. This Heart is repeatedly wounded with the impossibility to achieve such a forgiveness. In this life we cannot square the circle and make up the difference between what appears irrevocably lost and what is owed.

The Heart (In)Justice has confused surrender with powerlessness. It sees our participation in Christ's suffering as a covering over of trespasses. It views Christianity as a facile harmony with little to offer but trading forms of resignation and rage. This Heart reduces Christ's forgiveness on the cross to all too human conceptions of forgiveness that can never complete the task. It sees Christ as a *man*, not fully God and fully man. It forgets what Christ can do.

> The cross is certainly a most violent image, putting suffering and death before us with a rude emphasis; and I can understand the preference of many for the serene Buddha, lifting the finger of meditation and profound counsel, and freeing the soul by the sheer force of knowledge and of sweet reason. Nevertheless, I am not sorry to have been born a Christian: for the soul cannot be really freed except by ceasing to live; and it is whilst we still exist, not after we are dead to existence, that we need counsel. It is therefore the crucified spirit, not the liberated spirit, that is our true master. . . . The knowledge that existence can manifest but cannot retain

Mistaken Views on the Impossibility of Forgiveness

the good reconciles us at once to living and to dying. That, I think, is the wisdom of the Cross.
—George Santayana, *Soliloquies in England*

4

The Power of Christ's Forgiveness

Crystal Fire, **by Carol Scott**

The Power of Christ's Forgiveness

There is something to the sound of metal hitting the air, released from its
    coverall
I can hear it now

I feel the end nearing but I am washed in love
This is the end bearing down but I could not love you more
Every teardrop oceanic tides drowning infinite gods

This sense of you, the held relief of you is made on another ground
It wraps its arms and becomes All Soul

But there is something lurking in the air, cold around my features pressed
    belly of the beast
Of tales long ago and older demons hollowed and alive

If only your eyes could take me and remove the end, the slide of metal and
    neck
Young deer safe in the hide

What is it about sensation and selection?
The solidified drawn curtain, the shifting seats, the spectators and the
    spectral
Under the axe of one centurion

What is it about knowing without power?
The senses never marred with age and never graceless remains
I could not love you more than at that moment when . . . but my head is
    nowhere to be found

Some weight I cannot know has laid on my chest, an instrument of time
Reminded fabrics rough yet smooth

In April love was born and love died, in April I confide my heart now
    everywhere
In the sheets, in the baking scents, in the way your kiss comes on steep
Stronger than the cathedral bell, ringing through me in rainfall sweet

The Impossible Possibility

I cry for you my love, cry because time cannot remain our friend
If only my tears were graces and they could fly as angel in the night

If only my tears were a single grace
They are only the water and the salt now animating my body
My tears must be my soul for I cannot take another April when love was born and love died

I cry for you my love, I am made of tears cascading for you, tasting of the time of your lips
When the sense of you worked into me another ground
Rolling hill and vale and you became All Soul, but soon the angel will be gone
For we cannot live on weeping

—"The Axe and Tear," by Caitlin Smith Gilson

It is true that no future enjoyment on earth can make up for the evils that destroy a life. But heaven does not work in this way. Our earthly relationships already give us glimpses of the distinct heavenly direction at work. We are always in relation to others. We give and receive ourselves and become who we are in that relationship stretched over time. We interiorize not only our own experiences of life but the experience of others who have experienced us. The more deeply we follow this thread, the closer we realize Christ is the root of it all. Our closeness in friendship and in love includes an interiorization of the other person and an exteriorization of what we have taken in and contributed to the conversation. Each of us is breathing in and out the spirit of the other.

Human relationships are our greatest earthly clue to divine justice. Christ has loved us before the foundation of the world. He made the deepest human relationship possible. We become the most profound sense of ourselves in interiorizing and exteriorizing our relationship to Christ. When we love Christ and He loves us, throughout our lives we ourselves become a divine stretching of love. Heaven is not only a union of ourselves with other people, fulfilling our anticipation of supreme joy and love, but heaven accomplishes this love by way of a spiraling reversal that works through time, history, memory, into the very heart of Christ Himself. Every one of our losses He bears. Every one of our failures is consumed within His flesh. Every earthly incompletion nailed to the tree. Through Christ we are loved with the power *before* the foundation of the world. Who we are is anchored in that power.

When our persons are revealed in the love before the foundation of the world, everything spirals and turns in a new direction of recovery and transcendence. Not only are our failures overcome but even our achievements are stripped bare. All achievements are revealed also as failures to achieve. Every saint is also revealed to be a sinner. Every gain revealed as loss and every loss revealed as gain. All together becoming a chorus unearthing our transcendent need for Christ to overcome the world. Christ turns everything upside down, so that it can be made anew. Christ empties Himself in love for us.

Christ's self-emptying justice is not like any earthly justice. It is not "the transgression has been done, now let's scramble to figure out how to make it better," as is the case in earthly justice. Christ's justice is: "the transgression has been done but everything occurs on the body of existence itself." Christ *is* Existence Itself, for He is God. Christ's body is the very place where all human action, virtue, and vice occur. Christ is, again, Existence.

He empties Himself so completely in the incarnation and the passion. Christ therefore empties each of us—our sins, our failures—within Him as we are His other. Our emptying is simultaneously the power of His Love that overflows. Christ emptied Himself. This is existence that He is emptying, our sinful existence. In this emptying, we simultaneously overflow in His love. Christ is Love Itself. We finally, through grace, have a chance not only for earthly justice but a justice that is supernaturally merciful. In the only justice that can complete what is lost, we are remade in love, wholly born anew.

> "Truly, truly, I say to you, unless one is born again, he cannot see the kingdom of God." Nicodemus said to him, "How can a man be born when he is old? Can he enter a second time into his mother's womb and be born?" Jesus answered, "Truly, truly, I say to you, unless one is born of water and the Spirit, he cannot enter the kingdom of God. That which is born of the flesh is flesh, and that which is born of the Spirit is spirit. Do not marvel that I said to you, 'You must be born again.'"
> —John 3:15

Guilt and the Mystery of Forgiveness: Caligula and Aristotle

Our guilt is not limited and separated off into the lives of each person. Guilt *always* has an underlying reference to humanity as a whole. Each of us participates in this guilt.

> All men are jointly committed and jointly liable. Their common origin and their common goal account for this. A token of this, though not an explanation, is that we feel shaken and perplexed at the following thought, which seems absurd to our limited understanding: I am responsible for all the evil that is perpetrated in the world, unless I have done what I could to prevent it, even to the extent of sacrificing my life. I am guilty because I am alive and can continue to live while this is happening. Thus, criminal complicity takes hold of everyone for everything that happens. We must therefore speak of guilt in the wider sense of a guilt of human existence as such, and of guilt in the narrower sense of responsibility for a particular action. Where our own guilt is not limited to certain specific wrongdoings but, in a deeper sense, is found in the very nature of human existence, there the idea of guilt becomes truly inclusive.
> —Karl Jaspers, *The Tragic*

The Power of Christ's Forgiveness

No sin is done in isolation, and no goodness is done without communion. We are each revealing for others themselves and ourselves. Once this sinks in and lingers for a good while, the heart comes to realize its total responsibility for all actions. Each choice becomes coextensive with eternal judgment. We are to understand that if my brother has sinned then, in a way sacred and profound, I have sinned with him. If I have not done everything I can, then I am complicit in all sins of the world. But this structure of relationship as intrinsic and impossible obligation renders forgiveness too difficult to achieve, too painful to undertake. Forgiveness becomes too global and too intimate in one stroke of the brush. If all are complicit, who among us is capable of offering forgiveness? If we are permitted to offer forgiveness in the image and likeness of Christ, how can we if we are unable to put ourselves in contact with all the sins that surround us? Nor can we place ourselves completely within the will of another. Every saint is described as "another Christ." The saints know the literal preposterousness of the term. Human relationships place us squarely within the impossibility to complete forgiveness within our own powers.

Camus' Caligula is one such tragic figure who recognized the incongruity of existence. Lives are lost and little adds up. What is gained in this life is quicksand, escaping and consuming us before it is ever really ours. Rather than enter the dishonesty of a world of false harmony, of cheap forgiveness used to maintain a superficial polite society, Caligula chose madness. This choice is a forming of terrible calculating sanity, when faced with a world of dead ends. Caligula opts for the path of impossibility as impossible, unapproachable, yet devastatingly present. He sees it as the only source that could give genuine meaning. From there, he lives out its capriciousness, where the only rule is the arbitrary concatenation of events. And if he and others can endure this impossibility sufficiently, perhaps the impossible will transfigure them and give them happiness:

> And I'm resolved to change them.... I shall make this age of ours a kingly gift—the gift of equality. And when all is leveled out, when the impossible has come to Earth and the moon is in my hands—then, perhaps, I shall be transfigured, and the world renewed; then men will die no more and at last be happy.
> —Albert Camus, *Caligula*

Caligula has recognized the impossibility of forgiveness and embodies the three main alternatives (Promethean, Tragic, (In)Justice) which honestly acknowledge the incongruity at work in every second of life, and the impossible harmony heaven appears to offer. But then Caligula commits his sufferings to others, causing his subjects relentless and absurd humiliation and death. Caligula demands the reality of the impossible be present in every spontaneous action, calculated whim, and cruel command. The impossible must be in all the secret places of his heart and the hearts of others. Caligula never uses escapism. He confronts the abyss and knows that ineluctable impossibility guards the gate to everything meaningful and worthy of belief. Through reason and logic, Caligula takes the worst path before him: what is impossible, *as* impossibility, *is* impossible to achieve. Accept the absurd. There is nothing to be done but to endure or not to endure. This is the end of achievement, but not the end of heartache. Nearing his betrayal and assassination, he has neither expected nor achieved any of that impossibility. Caligula still hoped for it, as he hoped for the moon in his hands. All that remained in him was that wild unforgiving hope, or is that despair? He knowingly desires what he knows to be impossible and chases it until his demise. Still, Caligula calls out moments before his assassination that he has taken the wrong path:

> And I'm afraid. That's cruelest of all, after despising others, to find oneself as cowardly as they are. Still, no matter. Fear, too, has an end. Soon I shall attain that emptiness beyond all understanding, in which the heart has rest. Yet, really, it's quite simple. If I'd had the moon, if love were enough, all might have been different. But where could I quench this thirst? What human heart, what god, would have for me the depth of a great lake? [Kneeling, weeping] There's nothing in this world, or in the other, made to my stature. And yet I know, and you, too, know [still weeping, he stretches out his arms toward the mirror] that all I need is for the impossible to be. The impossible! I've searched for it at the confines of the world, in the secret places of my heart. I've stretched out my hands [his voice rises to a scream]; see, I stretch out my hands, but it's always you I find, you only, confronting me, and I've come to hate you. I have chosen a wrong path, a path that leads to nothing. My freedom isn't the right one.
> —Albert Camus, *Caligula*

How could Caligula consider the impossible a path and the *right* one? Our best intentions are always met with failure, failure to transform, failure to forgive into the bones. With Caligula, we are searching for something so much more than the virtue of magnanimity. For Aristotle, one of the chief signs of a magnanimous or high-minded person would be the way forgiveness is handled. This person is so wrapped up in his own transcendent likeness to the wisdom of the divine mind that it would be a contradiction to hold a grudge, to obsess on retribution. The trespasses of the inferior man are too trifling a project to consume one's time and energies. Forgiveness, for Aristotle, becomes more of a one-way affair. The high-minded person prefers to offer forgiveness and seeks never to be in a position to receive it. Forgiveness of a debt is a virtuous act, providing goodness, but the receiving of forgiveness only illustrates one's inferiority:

> He who received a good is inferior to the man who conferred it, and a high-minded man wishes to be superior. . . . It is the mark of the high-minded man, too, never, or hardly ever, to ask for help but to be of help to others readily. . . . Nor will he bear grudges; for it is the mark of a high-minded man not to bring up the past, especially what was bad, but rather to overlook this.
> —Aristotle, *Nichomachean Ethics*

The Aristotelian rationale for not seeking vengeance is not incompatible with the Christian understanding of forgiveness. Neither does it even come close to what is needed, desired, and made possible through Christ's sacrifice. In this one-way affair, there could never be friendship between the superior and inferior man, between the pardoner and the debtor, as Christ extends to us. When Christ becomes human, child, man, son, becoming one of us, He offers us friendship as well as salvation. Aristotle's forgiveness terminates in a one-way direction. The act ensures one's own so-called magnanimity but does not seek the better of the debtor. The education and virtue of the debtor is largely ignored. The debtor's moral and spiritual recovery is given the more peripheral attention when that degree of release or accord has been granted. The pardoning does not intend directly to promote the cultivation of the debtor's happiness and virtue. Again, we return to the one-way notion of forgiveness that does not reflect the incarnational offer of friendship Christ gives us. The forgiveness given by Aristotle's magnanimous person is more an indifference. It does not engage in the healing of the one forgiven for his or her good.

Forgiveness is redemptive only because it is simultaneously impossible. If this impossibility is not held central in all discussions, we have nowhere to direct ourselves except perpetual self-annihilation, hell. Forgiveness has *always* been about forgiving the unpardonable, the impossible, otherwise it is not the arduous act that Christ alone completed, in which all the glory and folly of humanity resides.

The Impossible Possibility

All the evils Caligula has done are far weightier than his final lines, which are just a glimmer of repentance: "I have chosen a wrong path, a path that leads to nothing. My freedom isn't the right one." Are we not taught, and rightly so, that actions speak louder than words? But here, with Caligula, we are presented with a predicament. The loss of the ability to love unreservedly. The eternally lost soul. Without forgiveness, there is hell, and we would not wish hell on our own worst enemy. If Caligula is unforgiven and unredeemed, he is eternally lost. Isn't that loss far weightier, and because we are all connected it includes each of us. If we take seriously the demands of human relationships, where no sin is done in isolation, the loss of just one soul to hell is never the loss of one soul. If we have not done all we can, and we never achieve all that the day demands, then we are complicit in each other's sins. To fail to forgive or to be forgiven means that we have lost the ability to love and be loved unreservedly. Should Christ refuse to forgive us, being one with us, then all would amount to nothing in the end. Just as Caligula in his madness foresaw. How do we manage this forgiveness genuinely, a forgiveness that appears to violate all logic and common sense? It appears that a true remission of sins may be the most beautiful act, and yet the most incommensurate in all existence. Life does not add up, it never has.

> Being genuinely good would mean that we would accomplish in every hour what that hour required, and thus life would ascend to the fullness of its achievement and perfection as called for by God. What is not done now cannot, however, be made good later on, because every hour comes but once, and the next has, once again, its own demands. What becomes of the gaps and voids in this continually passing life? And how do things stand with what has been done wrong? . . . What has been done rests in being. What will become of that when time has run out and man can do nothing more?
> —Romano Guardini in Hans Urs von Balthasar, *Dare We Hope*

5

Christ's Saving Love in His Seven Last Words

The Dying God, by Carol Scott

The Impossible Possibility

I sense in the late nights I am not long for this world
Sometimes I know I am not long for this place, the person of my body, this
    world
Other times I think I may live forever, but my eyes have a memory to them
They chase the night as last call, last drink, last things, I do not see very well
I do not know if I am looking at you, but I can close my eyes and see you
The day we made love on the floor, long words of you written across my body
They are always there, press my skin and you can feel them suspended
Sometimes the mind scatters the dust, I think of poured syrup, the joys you
    knew
It has all been a jar of compressed maple, it all has a scent to me these years
You always smelled of fresh soap, so clean, a kind of innocence wafting in pain
I could never take your tears, I have never walked in deep forest, it frightens me
I can do city blocks in rain, I know I am not long for this world, I imagine the
    leaves give way
To some hidden depth, I do not want you to go, do not bury me in the forest, far
    away
I want to be sugar and light and morning, to live forever, I think I will live
    forever
Sometimes though I know my time is gone
I lost something precious today, a token, a remnant of floors and sights
So many insights of the mind, scanning the emptied earth, a locket of eternal life
I am not long for this time, till death parts the waves, crashing into the rocks
The winter's bay where I could see your breath
God I love that you have lived and breathed, break me all over again
I am not long for this day for this night, when I walk and taste the sap
Will it be heaven sent, and you dear one, you resting close by

    —"My Secret," by Caitlin Smith Gilson

Is our claim that forgiveness is impossible except through Christ one that emaciates forgiveness? The Word is inescapable: only say the word and my soul shall be healed. One may contend that forgiveness is now too rare, restricted, and removed from any natural context. That it is placed instead within the realm of theological belief. And such sequestering injures the universality in which all persons are called. But we argue to the contrary. Without Christ's sacrifice, revealing the infinite in the finite, the universality of forgiveness would be a non-redemptive theoretical idea. The forgiveness we seek is the one that enables us to co-create paradise with Christ. Christ's self-emptying alone universalizes forgiveness within the world. Forgiveness hinges entirely on His justice and mercy, and it is revealed to us in the seven sayings of Christ on the cross.

Father, Forgive Them, for They Know Not What They Do

> It remains a source of comfort for all times and for all people that both in the case of those who genuinely did not know (his executioners) and in the case of those who did know (the people who condemned him), the Lord makes ignorance the motive for his plea for forgiveness: he sees it as a door that can open us to conversion.
> —Pope Benedict XVI, *Jesus of Nazareth II*

Christ's entire self-emptying is the key to forgiving our sins. His totalizing sacrifice allows our most confused desires for forgiveness to be clarified and seen. Christ enters the depths of the impossible and the failed, and He subsumes that ignorance, impossibility, and failure within human language in its pure form spoken by God as Word. Christ as the Word can speak the Word that can overcome the world and recover what is lost. This is meant on every level of existence. "We do not know what we do" not only signifies the moral level of ignorance and injustice. Christ's first saying on the cross has a twofold significance within salvation. It also evokes the union of our body and soul. As intellectual beings made in the image and likeness of God, we are not fully *in* time. Human knowledge means that our souls act from eternity when they act in time. And because it is our nature to be unified to a body, we are naturally in and *not* in time in every act of knowledge. Human beings act from eternity as united to their intellectual soul that, as the guide of the body, protracts that eternity into the moving image of each human person. This is why our embodiment created by and dependent on God allows each of us to be individuals. This longer way is the moving image of eternity discovered in the experience of time. We can be the moving image of eternity because our spiritual nature directs us to one end as truly satisfying, namely heaven. But what happens when, through sin, we sever our relationship with the eternal, and thwart that grace? We are looking through the glass darkly, and unable to know what we truly desire. We can forsake our happiness to such finality as death, and we are unable to recover it. We are the first cause of the loss of grace in our lives, but God is always the first to give that grace and remove the ignorance we placed upon ourselves.

Today You Will Be with Me in Paradise

> We already know from the *Night of the Senses* that a time arrives at which all taste for spiritual exercises as well as for all terrestrial things is taken away from the soul. She is put into total darkness and emptiness. Absolutely nothing that might give her a hold is left to her anymore except faith. Faith sets Christ before her eyes: the poor, humiliated, crucified one, who is abandoned on the cross even by his heavenly Father. In his poverty and abandonment, she rediscovers herself.
> —St. Edith Stein, *The Science of the Cross*

Christ suffered for us with an arduous, personal, and sacrificial love. His martyrdom enabled us to become united with Him through His body. We recover and receive our redeeming personhood through His self-emptying. United to Christ in the passion we enter the homelessness where all unremitted sins reside, where the impossibility to undo our trespasses devours everything it caresses. Through Him, we are forgiven because we know not, nor could we conceive the terror of what we have done. We are redeemed through Him Who has unraveled sin to its core. He took us in and became Death itself. Christ made what was once impossible to survive and the enemy of life, death, the threshold to the heaven that He is. When we hide in Christ's wounds, we will be with Him in paradise.

Woman, Behold, Your Son! Behold, Your Mother!

> She too had gone up her Calvary.
> She too had gone up and up
> In the general confusion, lagging a little behind . . .
> She wept and wept under a big linen veil.
> A big blue veil . . .
> A little faded.—
> She wept as it will never be granted to a woman to weep.
> As it will never be asked
> Of a woman to weep on this earth.
> —Charles Péguy, *The Passion of Our Lady*

Christ's self-emptying left Himself stranded within partial knowledge, incomplete understandings, unfinished actions, and abandonment from the Father. Christ took on the history of our fallenness, of our failed loves, and recovered them within His body. He transformed our dead-ends into a unity, where each may participate in bearing Christ for the other. Each of us is called to love with the bond of mother and child. The bond that brings the divine into the world. The mother is pro-creative, the prime participant in God's bringing of the life of love into the world. We are called to this bond with each other universally. We can now achieve this unity through Christ Who makes up what we lack. Marvelously, we get to participate in filling up those wounds of Christ, helping to form the very architecture of heaven. For Christ *is* heaven itself.

> Now I rejoice in my sufferings for your sake, and in my flesh I am filling up what is lacking in Christ's afflictions for the sake of his body, that is, the church.
> —Colossians 1:24

My God, My God, Why Have You Forsaken Me?

> Both robbers glared at me with glassy eyes; their foreheads glowed as waxen foreheads should—and yet the eyes of Christ: gulf-deep, death-dark, held such an eerie—almost living—spark, that all my blood rushed hotly toward my heart: the eyelids of the waxen God had been opening wide, then shutting—bluish-thin; quietly rose, and quietly sank in his slight, hurt chest; the pale lips came apart as if to form a word that, sick with aching, now forced its way through rows of ivory: "Why has thou, oh my God, forsaken me?" And as I heard him, by that dark word shaken, that word whose meaning could not be mistaken and stood, and stood, and nothing else could see,—then lightly from the Crucifixion Tree he loosed his white hands, groaning: "I am he."
> —Rainer Maria Rilke, *Visions of Christ*

Christ's divine justice surrendered His omnipotence to the Father. This act of self-emptying prefigured the lengths and total risk of forgiveness within the rescue mission. He placed Himself completely at the will of the supreme Father. Christ experienced the profound unnaturalness of the human body subjected to death through sin. Christ experienced the extreme suffering of souls which can persist but do so far outside the good of their natures. The piercing of the nails, the lancing of the flesh, the crown of thorns, all these violations of His once inviolate Being. Christ experienced the terrible, unimaginable suffering of the torn separation, the rupture across all history and time, of the human body and soul. "Father, forgive them, for they know what they have do." Now Christ must bear the impossible weight of the justice needed for forgiveness. He must complete what we have done to ourselves, to our bodies and souls in time and for all time. Only in Christ do we receive the forgiveness that recovers the unity of body and soul we hope to gain, glorified in the resurrection.

I Thirst

Our Lord's passion prefigured the riskiest and most distressing of leaps by entering into flesh, blood, and time. This is not a forgiveness for the few, it is for the many, offered for all. Every last drop of His substance flows forth and Christ is exsanguinated. He is poured out like water, and He thirsts because of it. He has entered nothing by His own self-emptying. Let us never forget how impossible forgiveness is without the God-Man's total gift. Christ thirsts for the world in its un-redeemability, which demands more and more of His water and blood.

> I am poured out like water, and all my bones are out of joint: my heart is like wax; it is melted in the midst of my bowels. My strength is dried up like a potsherd; and my tongue cleaves to my jaws; and thou hast brought me into the dust of death.
> —Psalm 22:14–15

It Is Finished

In His *"It is finished,"* Christ completes His supremely loving self-emptying. He illuminates the hidden Trinity. He grants us sight of the third person, the Holy Spirit, who is to be our Helper on earth. Christ has paid our debt, completed the architecture of salvation. In self-emptying, He breathes His last breath, and the breath of the Holy Spirit is upon us. This completion enables us to be alive with the Holy Spirit. Christ's *"It is finished"* fulfills the Old Testament:

> And it shall come to pass afterward, that I will pour out my spirit upon all flesh; and your sons and your daughters shall

prophesy, your old men shall dream dreams, your young men shall
see visions.
—Joel 2:28

"It is finished" also prefigures why, after His resurrection, Christ tells His flock:

> And I will ask the Father, and he will give you another Helper, to be with you forever, even the Spirit of truth, whom the world cannot receive, because it neither sees him nor knows him. You know him, for he dwells with you and will be in you.
> —John 14:16–17

Father, into Your Hands I Commend My Spirit

Heaven truly visited the earth. It remains in the earth in the body of the church, in us through the Holy Spirit permeating each of us with gifts, and in heaven with Christ seated at the right hand of the Father. In His last word, Christ's *self-emptying* splendor completes what His first saying sets out to do: "Father, forgive them, for they know not what they do." Now we know what we *must* do. We must commend everything we are, as Christ has already done for us. We must commend our body and soul to God the Father. Human forgiveness is an act of loving self-emptying trust. "If you really believe, then all corrects itself." This is an impossible foundation but the impossible has occurred and died and been resurrected for us. The impossible but real God-Man is in us. Christ is through us, in every bone, flesh, blood, heart, spirit, soul, and mind that constitutes our being. We are permeated with the impossible and this is *why* we can truly forgive! We live on the dying earth and yet simultaneously possess the eternalizing gate to heaven. Christ's completion of forgiveness is the astonishing foundation in which there is finally the spoken word—"only say the word and I shall be healed"—in which sins can be remitted. All that lostness, emptiness, and abandoning of ourselves can become the fullness and abundance of new life. The truly transformative relationship, the only one where I am completely united to another person, is in the forgiveness that is one with Christ's martyrological love.

Forgiveness is both impossible and necessary. This is the heart of Christ's ever-present *self-emptying* in every act of transubstantiation and communion. His blood and water flow eternally bearing these tensions of Good Friday and Easter Sunday, of time and eternity, of hell overcome and heaven rejoiced. Through His incarnation, heaven has visited earth and opened the door to the ultimate and astonishing remission of sins. If we are to achieve forgiveness, it works in reverse, by debriding every event of its finality, incompletion, failure, and even achievement. All events are subordinated to Christ. They are fulfilled *only* in Christ. He has emptied Himself and completed within His flesh every genuine desire of every failed love. When we unite with His body, we enter heaven on earth. Even with all our sinfulness, we experience the poignant beauty that cleanses the impossible of its impossibility. Again: "If we really believe, then all corrects itself." This is the endlessly giving power Christ offers to the faithful when He gave us Himself, emptied on the cross, and in His glorified body in the resurrection.

We interiorize and exteriorize the God-Man within us so that if we truly believe, "all will be corrected." This is the radical blessing of being in the image and likeness of Christ. Belief must become a co-created gift, a divine self-emptying within us, transforming us, completing what is within us perpetually incomplete. Only then are we able to forgive and be forgiven.

> "Son," he said, "ye cannot in your present state understand eternity": when Anodos looked through the door of the Timeless he brought no message back. But ye can get some likeness of it if ye say that both good and evil, when they are full grown, become retrospective. Not only this valley but all their earthly past will have been Heaven to those who are saved. Not only the twilight in that town, but all their life on Earth too, will then be seen by the damned to have been Hell. That is what mortals misunderstand. They say of some temporal suffering, "No future bliss can make up for it," not knowing that Heaven, once attained, will work backwards and turn even that agony into a glory. And of some sinful pleasure they say "let me have but *this* and I'll take the consequences": little dreaming how damnation will spread back and back into their past and contaminate the pleasure of the sin. Both processes begin even before death. The good man's past begins to change so that his forgiven sins and remembered sorrows take on the quality of Heaven: the bad man's past already conforms to his badness and is filled only with dreariness. And that is why, at the end of all things, when the sun rises here and the twilight turns to blackness down there, the Blessed will say "We have never lived anywhere except in Heaven," and the Lost, "We were always in Hell." And both will speak truly.
> —C. S. Lewis, *The Great Divorce*

Goodbye Rain, by Carol Scott

The Impossible Possibility

Every day since you were born has been Spring, no matter the sorrow

The loss and keeping, the stretched force of fates, my arms open and closing
Down into your home and mine

It is always forever Spring my words, their speaking is Spring, upon your look and touch
The light will never end, green covers the ground in Spring

I am the old of endless tumbling, of earth giving over its song
It may be winter but I am never lost
You are the long long days of Spring, the sun will never fail us
Your warmth that day, the day you were born held itself to me and I was the unknowing one

You were the first time I was, in the time of my Spring, the time that I became yours

See the hollow ahead, a road with wild trees, all lush canopies and hedges
In Spring, there are bushes of honeysuckle, their scent is the promise of an oil sweet
It tells you that I am near, it will always be that way
My kisses cover you as honeysuckle when you sleep and sleep and wake and sleep

My heart is everything that Spring is, do you sight the blossoms bright
Popping pinks, your cheekbones, your soft face unmarred by salt and age
Your roundness was that color the day you were made in my arms
Which is every day when I am everything that Spring is

Remember I am always with you, forever thinking, placing my soul in the shade
In the sun heading your way, reflecting the days the earth will never end
It will never end and I love you

I love you with everything that is the best in me, and I borrow more from the gods
More love and more Spring and more sun
Just to raid your heart with your fragrance that you give me that day long ago

The God who made you kneaded you into me before I was born
Honeysuckle scent and long rays of sunshine that first day of May

   —"Every Day Since You Were Born," by Caitlin Smith Gilson

Bibliography

Aeschylus, Sophocles, and Euripides. *The Greek Plays: Sixteen Plays by Aeschylus, Sophocles, and Euripides*. Translated by Mary Lefkowitz and James Romm. New York: Modern Library, 2017.
Anselm. *The Devotions of St. Anselm*. Edited by C. C. J. Webb. London: Methuen, 1903.
Aquinas, Thomas. *De Veritate*. Translated by Robert W. Mulligan. Chicago: Regnery, 1952.
———. *In Librum Beati Dionysii de Divinis Nominibus Expositio*. Edited by C. Pera and C. Mazzantini. Turin: Marietti, 1950.
———. *Meditations for Lent*. Translated by Philip Hughes. London: Sheed and Ward, 1937.
———. *On Being and Essence (De Ente et Essentia)*. Translated by Armand Maurer. Toronto: Pontifical Institute of Mediaeval Studies, 1949.
———. *Summa Contra Gentiles*. Translated by James F. Anderson. South Bend, IN: University of Notre Dame Press, 1992.
———. *Summa Theologiae*. Edited by Thomas Gilby. New York: Cambridge University Press, 1967.
Aristotle. *The Basic Works of Aristotle*. Edited by R. McKeon. New York: Random House, 1941.
Augustine. *City of God*. Edited by Vernon Bourke. New York: Image, 1958.
———. *Confessions*. Translated by Henry Chadwick. New York: Oxford University Press, 1998.
Balthasar, Hans Urs von. *The Christian and Anxiety*. San Francisco: Ignatius, 2000.
———. *Dare We Hope That All Men Be Saved? With a Short Discourse on Hell*. San Francisco: Ignatius, 2014.
———. *Love Alone Is Credible*. Translated by D. C. Schindler. San Francisco: Ignatius, 2004.
Behr, John. *The Mystery of Christ: Life in Death*. Yonkers, NY: St Vladimir's Seminary Press, 2006.
Belloc, Hilaire. *A Conversation with an Angel: And Other Essays*. New York: Harper, 1929.
———. *The Path to Rome*. London: Allen and Unwin, 1916.
Bernard of Clairvaux. *Bernard of Clairvaux: Selected Works*. Translated by Gillian Rosemary Evans. New York: Paulist, 1987.
Callard, Agnes. "The Philosophy of Anger." *Boston Review: A Political and Literary Forum* (April 22, 2020).
Camus, Albert. *Caligula and Three Other Plays*. Translated by Stuart Gilbert. New York: Vintage, 1962.

Bibliography

Catholic Church. *Catechism of the Catholic Church*. Vatican City: Libreria Editrice Vaticana, 2000.

———. *The Office for the Dead: According to the Roman Breviary, Missal and Ritual*. Toronto: Gale, 2010.

Chekhov, Anton. *The Lady with the Little Dog and Other Stories, 1896–1904*. Translated by Ronald Wilks. London: Penguin, 2002.

Chesterton, G. K. *The Collected Works of G. K. Chesterton, Volume 1: Heretics, Orthodoxy, the Blatchford Controversies*. San Francisco: Ignatius, 1986.

———. *The Everlasting Man*. San Francisco: Ignatius, 1993.

———. "Jesus or Christ." *The Hibbert Journal* (1909) 746–58.

———. *A Miscellany of Men*. New York: Dodd, Mead and Company, 1912.

Dante Alighieri. *The Divine Comedy* (The Inferno, The Purgatorio, The Paradiso). Translated by John Ciardi. New York: NAL Trade, 2003.

———. *La Vita Nuova*. Translated by David Slavitt. Cambridge: Harvard University Press, 2010.

Debout, Jacques. *My Sins of Omission*. Translated by J. F. Scanlan. London: Sands, 1930.

De Lubac, Henri. *Catholicism: Christ and the Common Destiny of Man*. Translated by Lancelot C. Sheppard and Elizabeth Englund. San Francisco: Ignatius, 1988.

———. *The Drama of Atheistic Humanism*. Translated by Mark Sebanc. San Francisco: Ignatius, 1995.

Derrida, Jacques. *The Gift of Death*. Translated by David Wills. Chicago: University of Chicago Press, 1995.

Desmond, William. *The Gift of Beauty and the Passion of Being: On the Threshold between the Aesthetic and the Religious*. Veritas. Eugene, OR: Cascade, 2018.

Dostoevsky, Fyodor. *The Brothers Karamazov*. Translated by Richard Pevear and Larissa Volokhonsky. New York: Farrar, Straus and Giroux, 1990.

The Douay-Rheims New Testament of Our Lord and Savior Jesus Christ. Compiled by Rev. George Leo Haydock. Monrovia, Liberia: Catholic Treasures, 1991.

The Douay-Rheims Old Testament of the Holy Catholic Bible. Compiled by Rev. George Leo Haydock. Monrovia, Liberia: Catholic Treasures, 1992.

Eliot, T. S. *T. S. Eliot: Collected Poems, 1909–1962*. Orlando: Harcourt, 1991.

Engelland, Chad. *Phenomenology*. Cambridge: MIT Press, 2020.

Gilson, Caitlin Smith. *Immediacy and Meaning: J. K. Huysmans and the Immemorial Origin of Metaphysics*. London: Bloomsbury, 2018.

———. *Metaphysical Presuppositions of Being-in-the-World: A Confrontation between St. Thomas Aquinas and Martin Heidegger*. New York: Continuum, 2010.

———. *The Philosophical Question of Christ*. London: Bloomsbury, 2014.

———. *The Political Dialogue of Nature and Grace: Toward a Phenomenology of Chaste Anarchism*. London: Bloomsbury, 2015.

———. *Subordinated Ethics: Natural Law and Moral Miscellany in Aquinas and Dostoyevsky*. Eugene, OR: Cascade, 2020.

Gilson, Étienne. *The Elements of Christian Philosophy*. New York: Mentor Omega, 1963.

Girard, René. *Things Hidden since the Foundation of the World*. Translated by Stephen Bann and Michael Metteer. Stanford, CA: Stanford University Press, 1987.

———. *Violence and the Sacred*. Translated by Patrick Gregory. Baltimore: Johns Hopkins University, 1979.

Guardini, R. *Pascal for Our Time*. Translated by Brian Thompson. New York: Herder, 1966.

BIBLIOGRAPHY

Heidegger, Martin. *The Phenomenology of Religious Life*. Translated by Matthias Fritsch and Jennifer Anna Gosetti-Ferenci. Bloomington, IN: Indiana University Press, 2010.

———. *Poetry, Language, Thought*. Translated by Albert Hofstadter. New York: Harper and Row, 1971.

Hugo, Victor. "La Conscience." *La Légende des Siècles*. Translated by Dublin University Magazine. https://www.gutenberg.org/files/8775/8775-h/8775-h.htm.

Huizinga, Johan. *The Waning of the Middle Ages*. Mineola, NY: Dover, 2013.

Huysmans, Joris Karl. *The Oblate*. Translated by Edward Perceval. London: Kegan Paul, 1918.

Jacobse, Johannes. "Eugene Ionesco and the Elder on Mount Athos." Orthodox Christianity Then and Now, May 23, 2011. https://www.johnsanidopoulos.com/2011/05/eugene-ionesco-and-elder-on-mount-athos.html

Jaeger, Werner. *Theology of the Early Greek Philosophers*. New York: Oxford University Press, 1947.

Jaspers, Karl. *Philosophical Faith and Revelation*. Translated by E. B. Ashton. New York: Harper and Row, 1967.

John of the Cross. *The Collected Works of St. John of the Cross*. Translated by Kieran Kavanaugh and Otilio Rodriguez. Washington, DC: ICS, 1991.

———. *A Spiritual Canticle of the Soul and the Bridegroom Christ*. Translated by David Lewis. Grand Rapids: Christian Classics Ethereal Library, 2000.

Journet, Charles. *The Meaning of Grace*. Glen Rock, NJ: Paulist, 1962.

Julian of Norwich. *Revelations of Divine Love: Short Text and Long Text*. Translated by Elizabeth Spearing. London: Penguin, 1988.

Kierkegaard, Søren. *The Essential Kierkegaard*. Edited by Howard V. Hong and Edna H. Hong. Princeton, NJ: Princeton University Press, 2000.

———. *Works of Love*. Translated by Howard V. Hong and Edna H. Hong. New York: Harper, 2009.

Kreeft, Peter. *Everything You Wanted to Know about Heaven but Never Dreamed of Asking*. San Francisco: Ignatius, 1990.

Levinas, Emmanuel. *Emmanuel Levinas: Basic Philosophical Writings*. Edited by Adriaan T. Peperzak, Simon Critchley, and Robert Bernasconi. Bloomington, IN: Indiana University Press, 1996.

Lewis, C. S. *The Abolition of Man*. New York: Harper, 2001.

———. *The Chronicles of Narnia*. New York: Harper, 2004.

———. *C. S. Lewis Signature Classics: Mere Christianity, The Screwtape Letters, A Grief Observed, The Problem of Pain, Miracles, and The Great Divorce*. New York: Harper, 2001.

———. *The Four Loves*. New York: Harper, 2001.

———. *A Grief Observed*. New York: Harper, 2001.

———. *Till We Have Faces: A Myth Retold*. New York: Harper, 1984.

———. *The Weight of Glory and Other Addresses*. New York: Harper, 2001.

Lowry, Rich. "The Humiliating Art of the Woke Apology." *National Review*, February 8, 2021. https://www.nationalreview.com/corner/the-humiliating-art-of-the-woke-apology/

Marion, Jean Luc. *God without Being*. Chicago: University of Chicago Press, 1995.

Maritain, Jacques. *Approaches to God*. Translated by Peter O'Reilly. New York: Harper, 1954.

Bibliography

———. *God and the Permission of Evil*. Translated by Joseph W. Evans. Milwaukee: Bruce, 1966.

———. *The Grace and Humanity of Jesus Christ*. Translated by Joseph W. Evans. New York: Herder and Herder, 1969.

———. *The Peasant of the Garonne: An Old Layman Questions Himself about the Present Time*. Translated by Michael Cuddihy and Elizabeth Hughes. Reprint, Eugene, OR: Wipf & Stock, 2013.

Mauriac, Francois. *The Inner Presence: Recollection of My Spiritual Life*. Indianapolis: Bobbs-Merrill, 1968.

Meister Eckhart. *Breakthrough: Meister Eckhart's Creation Spirituality in New Translation*. Translated by Matthew Fox. Garden City, NY: Image, 1980.

Milton, John. *Paradise Lost*. Edited by Roy C. Flannagan. New York: Dover, 2005.

Newman, John Henry. *The Apologia Pro Vita Sua*. New York: Norton, 1968.

———. *Meditations and Devotions*. London: Longmans, 1933.

Nietzsche, Friedrich. *Basic Writings*. Translated by Walter Kaufmann. New York: Modern Library, 2000.

Nussbaum, Martha. *Anger and Forgiveness: Resentment, Generosity, Justice*. Oxford: Oxford University Press, 2016.

O'Connor, Flannery. *A Prayer Journal*. Edited by W. A. Sessions. New York: Farrar, Straus and Giroux, 2013.

O'Regan, Cyril. *The Anatomy of Misremembering*. New York: Herder, 2014.

———. *Theology and the Spaces Apocalyptic*. Milwaukee: Marquette University Press, 2009.

Pascal, Blaise. *Pensees*. Translated by William Finlayson Trotter. New York: Dutton, 1958.

Pegis, Anton Charles. *At the Origins of the Thomistic Notion of Man*. New York: Macmillan, 1963.

———. *The Problem of the Soul in the 13th Century*. Toronto: Pontifical Institute of Mediaeval Studies, 1934.

Péguy, Charles. *Basic Verities*. Translated by Ann Green and Julian Green. New York: Pantheon, 1943.

———. *God Speaks: Religious Poetry*. Translated by Julian Green. New York: Pantheon, 1945.

———. *Man and Saints*. Translated by Julian Green. New York: Pantheon, 1944.

———. *The Mystery of the Holy Innocents and Other Poems*. Translated by Pansy Pakenham. Reprint, Eugene, OR: Wipf & Stock, 2018.

———. *Notre Patrie*. Paris: Payen, 1905.

———. *The Portal of the Mystery of Hope*. Translated by David L. Schindler, Jr. Grand Rapids: Eerdmans, 1996.

———. *Temporal and Eternal*. Translated by Alexandre Dru. Indianapolis: Liberty Fund, 2001.

Pieper, Josef. *Death and Immortality*. Translated by Richard Winston and Clara Winston. South Bend, IN: St. Augustine, 2000.

———. *Happiness and Contemplation*. South Bend, IN: St. Augustine, 1998.

Plato. *The Collected Dialogues of Plato, Including the Letters*. Edited by Edith Hamilton and Huntington Cairns. New York: Pantheon, 1961.

Pope Benedict XVI. *Deus Caritas Est*. Vatican City: Libreria Editrice Vaticana, 2005.

———. *Jesus of Nazareth, Part Two: Holy Week*. San Francisco: Ignatius, 2010.

Pope Francis. *Gaudete et Exsultate*. Vatican City: Libreria Editrice Vaticana, 2018.

BIBLIOGRAPHY

———. *Laudato Si*. Vatican City: Libreria Editrice Vaticana, 2015.

Pope Saint John Paul II. *Apostolic Letter Salvifici Doloris*. Vatican City: Libreria Editrice Vaticana, 1984.

———. *Dives in Misercordia*. Vatican City: Libreria Editrice Vaticana, 1980.

Pseudo-Dionysius. *Pseudo-Dionysius: The Complete Works*. Translated by Paul Rorem. Glen Rock, NJ: Paulist, 1987.

Rahner, Hugo. *Man at Play*. New York: Herder, 1967.

Rand, Ayn. *Atlas Shrugged*. Translated by Leonard Peikoff. New York: Penguin, 2005.

Ratzinger, Joseph. *On Conscience*. San Francisco: Ignatius, 2007.

Rilke, Rainier Maria. *The Book of Hours: Prayers to a Lowly God*. Translated by Annemarie Kidder. Evanston, IL: Northwestern University Press, 2001.

———. *The Complete French Poems*. Translated by A. Poulin, Jr. Saint Paul, MN: Graywolf, 2002.

———. *The Dark Interval: Letters on Loss, Grief, and Transformation*. Translated by Ulrich Baer. New York, Modern Library, 2018.

———. *The Duino Elegies*. Translated by Stephen Cohn. Evanston, IL: Northwestern University Press, 1989.

———. *Sonnets to Orpheus*. Translated by David Young. Hanover, NH: University Press of New England, 1987.

Santayana, George. *The Idea of Christ in the Gospels: Or God in Man, A Critical Essay*. New York: Scribner, 1946.

———. *Soliloquies in England and Later Soliloquies*. Ann Arbor, MI: University of Michigan, 1967.

Sartre, Jean Paul. *No Exit and Three Other Plays*. Translated by Stuart Gilbert. New York: Vintage, 1989.

Schindler, D. C. "Love and Beauty, the 'Forgotten Transcendental,' in Thomas Aquinas." *Communio* 44.2 (2017) 334–56.

Shakespeare, William. *The Complete Works of William Shakespeare*. Ware, UK: Wordsworth, 1996.

Shestov, Lev. *All Things Are Possible (Apotheosis of Groundlessness)*. Translated by Samuel Solomonovitch Kotelianksy. New York: McBride, 1920.

Solovyov, Vladimir. *The Meaning of Love*. Translated by Thomas R. Beyer. Hudson, NY: Lindisfarne, 1985.

Solzhenitsyn, Aleksandr. *The Gulag Archipelago: An Experiment in Literary Investigation*. Translated by Thomas P. Whitney. New York: HarperCollins, 1974.

Stein, Edith. *The Science of the Cross*. Translated by Josephine Koeppel. Washington, DC: ICS, 2002.

Teresa of Avila. *The Collected Works of St. Teresa of Avila, Volume 1*. Translated by Kieran Kavanaugh and Otilio Rodriguez. Washington, DC: ICS, 1976.

———. *The Collected Works of St. Teresa of Avila, Volume 2*. Translated by Kieran Kavanaugh and Otilio Rodriguez. Washington, DC: ICS, 1980.

Tertullian. *Tertullian's Treatise on the Incarnation De Carne Christi*. Edited by Ernest Evans. London: SPCK, 1956.

Traherne, Thomas. *Centuries of Meditations*. Edited by Bertram Dobell. London: Dobell, 1908.

Tolkien, J. R. R. *The Letters of J. R. R. Tolkien*. Edited by Christopher Humphries. New York: Houghton Mifflin Harcourt, 2000.

Bibliography

Unamuno, Miguel. *Our Lord Don Quixote: The Life of Don Quixote and Sancho with Related Essays*. Translated by Anthony Kerrigan. Princeton, NJ: Princeton University Press, 1967.

———. *Tragic Sense of Life*. Translated by J. E. Crawford Flitch. Mineola, NY: Dover, 1952.

Undset, Sigrid. *Kristin Lavransdatter II: The Wife*. Translated by Tiina Nunnally. New York: Penguin, 1999.

Vianney, John. *Little Catechism of the Cure of Ars*. Gastonia, NC: Tan, 1994.

Voegelin, Eric. *What Is History? And Other Late Unpublished Writings*. Collected Works Volume 28. Edited by Thomas A. Hollweck and Paul Caringella. Columbia, MO: University of Missouri Press, 1990.

Von Hildebrand, Dietrich. *Man, Woman and the Meaning of Love: God's Plan for Love, Marriage, Intimacy, and the Family*. Bedford, NH: Sophia Institute, 2002.

Von Speyr, Adrienne. *Confession*. San Francisco: Ignatius, 1985.

———. *The Cross: Word and Sacrament*. Translated by Graham Harrison. San Francisco: Ignatius, 2018.

Waugh, Evelyn. *Brideshead Revisited*. New York: Back Bay, 2008.

Williams, Charles. *The Figure of Beatrice*. Berkeley: Apocryphile, 2005.

Yeats, William Butler. *The Collected Poems of W. B. Yeats*. Edited by Richard J. Finnernan. New York: Scribner, 1996.

Index

Aeschylus, 56
Agape, 33
Aquinas, Saint Thomas, 7, 43
Aristotle, 64–68
Atonement, xii, 5, 7, 25, 31, 32, 41

Balthasar, Hans Urs von, 68

Caligula, xiii, 64–68
Camus, Albert, xiii, 65, 66
Chekhov, Anton, 17, 18, 37
Colossians, 73
Conscience, 2, 30, 37, 44
Creation, 6, 10, 41, 42, 47, 51

Debout, Jacques, 14
Dostoyevsky, Fyodor, 21, 30, 31

Eliot, Thomas Stearns, 56
Eros, 20, 33

Fortitude, 3, 33, 49

Gift, 6, 9, 10, 17, 23, 27, 32, 42, 43, 65, 74–76
Grace, 2, 6, 8–10, 16, 26, 29, 32, 33, 45, 55, 61, 62, 64, 71, 72
Guardini, Romano, 68

The Heart, xii, xiii, 13, 29, 41, 57–59, 65, 66, 75
Hell, 2, 6, 9, 10, 13, 17, 24–27, 29, 31, 34, 40–52, 54, 67, 68, 75, 76
Humility, 9, 31, 36, 46, 49, 54, 66, 72

Image and Likeness, 26, 34, 43, 65, 71, 76
Incarnation, 5, 8, 10, 11, 13, 51, 64, 67, 76
Ionesco, Eugene, 50, 51
Isaiah, 32

Jaspers, Karl, 64
Jesus, xii, 13, 27, 64, 71
Joel, 75
John, 64, 75
Justice, xi–xiii, 3–7, 9–10, 14, 17, 18, 21–35, 37, 38, 42–44, 46, 47, 51, 57, 58, 63–65, 68, 61, 74

Lewis, C.S., 10, 76
Longer Way, 8, 71
Lowry, Rich, 36
Luke, 5

Magnanimity, xiii, 38, 49, 66, 67
Martyrological, 72, 75
Matthew, 6, 9, 10, 17, 51, 55
Medea, xii, 15–39
Mercy, 5, 6, 8–10, 24, 26, 28, 38, 42, 43, 45, 46, 49, 51, 64, 71
Metaphysics, 47, 54

Nietzsche, Friedrich, xii, xiii, 18, 48–52

Péguy, Charles, 28, 72
Peter, 2, 5, 27
Pieper, Josef, 35
Pope Benedict XVI, 29, 71

Index

Pope Saint John Paul the Great, 5
Political, 24, 36, 65
Prayer, xii, 10, 14, 16, 43, 44, 51, 52
Prometheus, 44, 45, 56, 65
Proverbs, 34
Prudence, 7, 9, 32
Psalms, 74

Rilke, Rainer Maria, 73

Saint Edith Stein, 72
Saint Teresa of Avila, 45
Salvation, 3, 6, 9, 17, 18, 24, 27, 28, 42–47, 67, 71, 74
Santayana, George, 58, 59

Shakespeare, William, 57
Sin, xi, xii, 5, 7, 8, 10, 18, 22, 23, 29, 32, 38, 43, 44, 46, 47, 54, 65, 68, 72
Socratic, xiii

Tacitus, 25
Temperance, 9, 32, 33
Tragedy, 7, 19, 22, 57–59, 64, 65
Transcendent, 26, 32–34, 37, 47, 50, 55, 57, 63, 67
Transubstantiation, 75

Virtue, xii, 9, 20, 32–36, 63, 66, 67

www.ingramcontent.com/pod-product-compliance
Lightning Source LLC
Chambersburg PA
CBHW051133160426
43195CB00014B/2450